SIMOI

MW00478928

Simone de Beauvoir's groundbreaking work has transformed the way we think about gender and identity. Without her 1949 text *The Second Sex*, gender theory as we know it today would be unthinkable. A leading figure in French existentialism, Beauvoir's concepts of 'becoming woman' and of woman as absolute 'Other' are among the most influential ideas in feminist enquiry and debate.

This book guides the reader through the main areas of Simone de Beauvoir's thought, including:

* Existentialism and ethics
* Gender and feminism
* Literature and autobiography
* Sexuality, the body and ageing

Drawing upon Beauvoir's literary and theoretical texts, this is the essential guidebook for those approaching the work of this key thinker for the first time.

Ursula Tidd is a lecturer in French at the University of Manchester, and the author of *Simone de Beauvoir, Gender and Testimony* (1999).

ROUTLEDGE CRITICAL THINKERS

Series Editor: Robert Eaglestone, Royal Holloway, University of London

Routledge Critical Thinkers is a series of accessible introductions to key figures in contemporary critical thought.

With a unique focus on historical and intellectual contexts, each volume examines a key theorist's:

- significance
- motivation
- key ideas and their sources
- impact on other thinkers

Concluding with extensively annotated guides to further reading, *Routledge Critical Thinkers* are the student's passport to today's most exciting critical thought.

Already available:
Roland Barthes by Graham Allen
Jean Baudrillard by Richard J. Lane
Maurice Blanchot by Ullrich Haase and William Large
Judith Butler by Sara Salih
Gilles Deleuze by Claire Colebrook
Jacques Derrida by Nicholas Royle
Michel Foucault by Sara Mills
Sigmund Freud by Pamela Thurschwell
Martin Heidegger by Timothy Clark
Fredric Jameson by Adam Roberts
Julia Kristeva by Noëlle McAfee
Jean-François Lyotard by Simon Malpas
Paul de Man by Martin McQuillan
Friedrich Nietzsche by Lee Spinks
Paul Ricoeur by Karl Simms
Edward Said by Bill Ashcroft and Pal Ahluwalia
Gayatri Chakravorty Spivak by Stephen Morton

For further details on this series, see www.literature.routledge.com/rct

SIMONE DE BEAUVOIR

Ursula Tidd

Routledge
Taylor & Francis Group

LONDON AND NEW YORK

First published 2004
by Routledge
11 New Fetter Lane, London EC4P 4EE

Simultaneously published in the USA and Canada
by Routledge
29 West 35th Street, New York, NY 10001

Routledge is an imprint of the Taylor & Francis Group

Typeset in Perpetua by
Florence Production Ltd, Stoodleigh, Devon
Printed and bound in Great Britain by
TJ International Ltd, Padstow, Cornwall

British Library Cataloguing in Publication Data
A catalogue record for this book is available from the
British Library

Library of Congress Cataloging in Publication Data
Tidd, Ursula.
    Simone de Beauvoir / Ursula Tidd.
        p. cm. – (Routledge critical thinkers)
    Includes bibliographical references and index.
    1. Beauvoir, Simone de, 1908 – Criticism and interpretation.
    I. Title. II. Series.
    PQ2603.E362Z8868 2004
    848'.91409–dc21   2003011017

ISBN 0–415–26363–8 (hbk)
ISBN 0–415–26364–6 (pbk)

CONTENTS

SERIES EDITOR'S
PREFACE

The books in this series offer introductions to major critical thinkers who have influenced literary studies and the humanities. The *Routledge Critical Thinkers* series provides the books you can turn to first when a new name or concept appears in your studies.

Each book will equip you to approach a key thinker's original texts by explaining her or his key ideas, putting them into context and, perhaps most importantly, showing you why this thinker is considered to be significant. The emphasis is on concise, clearly written guides which do not presuppose a specialist knowledge. Although the focus is on particular figures, the series stresses that no critical thinker ever existed in a vacuum but, instead, emerged from a broader intellectual, cultural and social history. Finally, these books will act as a bridge between you and the thinker's original texts: not replacing them but rather complementing what she or he wrote.

These books are necessary for a number of reasons. In his 1997 autobiography, *Not Entitled*, the literary critic Frank Kermode wrote of a time in the 1960s:

> On beautiful summer lawns, young people lay together all night, recovering from their daytime exertions and listening to a troupe of Balinese musicians. Under their blankets or their sleeping bags, they would chat drowsily about the gurus of the time ... What they repeated was largely hearsay; hence my

lunchtime suggestion, quite impromptu, for a series of short, very cheap books offering authoritative but intelligible introductions to such figures.

There is still a need for 'authoritative and intelligible introductions'. But this series reflects a different world from the 1960s. New thinkers have emerged and the reputations of others have risen and fallen, as new research has developed. New methodologies and challenging ideas have spread through arts and humanities. The study of literature is no longer – if it ever was – simply the study and evaluation of poems, novels and plays. It is also the study of ideas, issues, and difficulties which arise in any literary text and in its interpretation. Other arts and humanities subjects have changed in analogous ways.

With these changes, new problems have emerged. The ideas and issues behind these radical changes in the humanities are often presented without reference to wider contexts or as theories which you can simply 'add on' to the texts you read. Certainly, there's nothing wrong with picking out selected ideas or using what comes to hand – indeed, some thinkers have argued that this is, in fact, all we can do. However, it is sometimes forgotten that each new idea comes from the pattern and development of somebody's thought and it is important to study the range and context of their ideas. Against theories 'floating in space', the *Routledge Critical Thinkers* series places key thinkers and their ideas firmly back in their contexts.

More than this, these books reflect the need to go back to the thinker's own texts and ideas. Every interpretation of an idea, even the most seemingly innocent one, offers its own 'spin', implicitly or explicitly. To read only books on a thinker, rather than texts by that thinker, is to deny yourself a chance of making up your own mind. Sometimes what makes a significant figure's work hard to approach is not so much its style or content as the feeling of not knowing where to start. The purpose of these books is to give you a 'way in' by offering an accessible overview of these thinkers' ideas and works and by guiding your further reading, starting with each thinker's own texts. To use a metaphor from the philosopher Ludwig Wittgenstein (1889–1951), these books are ladders, to be thrown away after you have climbed to the next level. Not only, then, do they equip you to approach new ideas, but also they empower you, by leading you back to the theorist's own texts and encouraging you to develop your own informed opinions.

Finally, these books are necessary because, just as intellectual needs have changed, the education systems around the world – the contexts in which introductory books are usually read – have changed radically, too. What was suitable for the minority higher education system of the 1960s is not suitable for the larger, wider, more diverse, high technology education systems of the twenty-first century. These changes call not just for new, up-to-date, introductions but new methods of presentation. The presentational aspects of *Routledge Critical Thinkers* have been developed with today's students in mind.

Each book in the series has a similar structure. They begin with a section offering an overview of the life and ideas of each thinker and explain why she or he is important. The central section of each book discusses the thinker's key ideas, their context, evolution and reception. Each book concludes with a survey of the thinker's impact, outlining how their ideas have been taken up and developed by others. In addition, there is a detailed final section suggesting and describing books for further reading. This is not a 'tacked-on' section but an integral part of each volume. In the first part of this section you will find brief descriptions of the thinker's key works: following this, information on the most useful critical works and, in some cases, on relevant websites. This section will guide you in your reading, enabling you to follow your interests and develop your own projects. Throughout each book, references are given in what is known as the Harvard system (the author and the date of a work cited are given in the text and you can look up the full details in the bibliography at the back). This offers a lot of information in very little space. The books also explain technical terms and use boxes to describe events or ideas in more detail, away from the main emphasis of the discussion. Boxes are also used at times to highlight definitions of terms frequently used or coined by a thinker. In this way, the boxes serve as a kind of glossary, easily identified when flicking through the book.

The thinkers in the series are 'critical' for three reasons. First, they are examined in the light of subjects which involve criticism: principally literary studies or English and cultural studies, but also other disciplines which rely on the criticism of books, ideas, theories and unquestioned assumptions. Second, they are critical because studying their work will provide you with a 'tool kit' for your own informed critical reading and thought, which will make you critical. Third, these thinkers are critical because they are crucially important: they deal with ideas and questions which can overturn conventional understandings of the world, of texts, of everything we take for granted, leaving us with a deeper understanding of what we already knew and with new ideas.

No introduction can tell you everything. However, by offering a way into critical thinking, this series hopes to begin to engage you in an activity which is productive, constructive and potentially life-changing.

ACKNOWLEDGEMENTS

I would like to thank Elizabeth Fallaize for her very helpful comments on an earlier draft of the manuscript. Thanks are also due to Bob Eaglestone and Liz Thompson for their incisive and good-humoured editorial work.

ABBREVIATIONS

References to books and essays by Simone de Beauvoir and Jean-Paul Sartre are abbreviated in the main text as indicated below; bibliographical information for these and other works by Beauvoir appear in the 'Further Reading' section. Sartre's work cited here can be found in full in the 'Works Cited' section. References in the text to other works by Beauvoir and Sartre and to works by other authors are provided using the Harvard (or author–date) system; full bibliographical details of these appear in the 'Works Cited' section.

ASD*	All Said and Done (1972)
BB*	'Brigitte Bardot and the Lolita syndrome' (1959)
BN*	Being and Nothingness (Sartre; 1943)
EA*	The Ethics of Ambiguity (1947)
FC*	The Force of Circumstance (1963)
LM	Littérature et métaphysique (1946)
MBS	'Must we burn Sade?' (1951–1952)
MDD*	Memoirs of a Dutiful Daughter (1958)
OA*	Old Age (1970)
PC	Pyrrhus et Cinéas (1944)
PL*	The Prime of Life (1960)
SS*	The Second Sex (1949)

* Page numbers relating to asterisked texts are taken from the translation rather than the original. See 'Further Reading' section for details.

WHY BEAUVOIR?

The French writer and feminist philosopher, Simone de Beauvoir (1908–1986), is one of the most important figures in twentieth-century thought. For most people, she is the author of *The Second Sex* (1949), the 'bible' of modern Western feminism. For others, she is a representative of the French post-war intelligentsia, associated with the philosophical movement of existentialism and with Jean-Paul Sartre. Beauvoir has had a major impact on the development of modern thought in feminist philosophy, in literary studies and in the social sciences throughout the world. A powerful intellectual role model for women in the twenty-first century, Beauvoir was an exacting and critical thinker, who provided an ethics relating to the brand of post-war atheistic existentialism associated with Sartre's *Being and Nothingness* (1943). This existentialist component of her work will be discussed in detail in Chapter 1. Since its publication in France in 1949, Beauvoir's *The Second Sex* has continued to shape debates and thinking about gender. Key feminist thinkers of recent decades, such as Luce Irigaray and Judith Butler, have acknowledged their intellectual debt to her work, even as they developed their own work on gender in quite different directions.

But Beauvoir saw herself primarily as a writer – of fiction, of philosophical and polemical essays, of auto/biography – and as an intellectual who, in the course of the Second World War, discovered a responsibility to history and to other people. Her writings fall into two main, but not necessarily distinct, categories: literature and philosophy. For much of her literary and philosophical work is interrelated in its practical and theoretical focus on similar sets of problems. For example, Beauvoir began to explore issues such as the nature of freedom and our responsibility to others in both her philosophical and literary writing of the 1940s.

At a general level, Beauvoir's writing is also infused with a fundamentally political consciousness, often analysing questions of power and freedom as they arise within the dynamics of interpersonal relationships as well as within a broader collective framework. Her political consciousness is integrally related to a specifically French notion of what it has meant to be a 'public intellectual' in the post war period, ready to speak out on the controversial questions of the time and, in Beauvoir's case, a 'committed' writer and thinker. Being 'engagée' or 'committed' in France in the 1940s and 1950s meant that she recognised the political and ethical significance and influence of the worldview presented in her literary writing and thought. One of Beauvoir's key ideas was the importance of 'situation' – understood in its existentialist sense as the relationship between our freedom to pursue a project and all the given aspects of the world which we have not chosen. This means that it is essential to situate the development of Beauvoir's own early thought in the first half of the twentieth century in France before we examine its key aspects in the subsequent chapters of this volume. No body of thought emerges in a political, philosophical or historical vacuum and this context will help you better understand the importance of Beauvoir's thought.

LIFE AND CONTEXTS

Simone de Beauvoir was born in Paris on 9 January 1908 into a conservative, bourgeois family. Her Parisian father, Georges, had trained as a lawyer, yet had a variety of jobs. An atheist who held extreme right-wing political views, he also acted in amateur theatre with her mother, Françoise, a strict Catholic from north-east France. At an early age Beauvoir experienced political and religious ideological clashes between her parents' value systems which, she would later claim in her autobiography, encouraged her to become a radical intellectual (MDD: 41). These clashes left her with an acute awareness of the relationship between ideology and its formative effects on subjectivity or how such value systems fundamentally shape our sense of identity and our ability to act in the world and in relation to other people.

Beauvoir trained to teach philosophy at the Sorbonne, an influential higher education college closely associated with the University of Paris. Sartre, her future partner, and most of his male contemporaries, however, studied at the prestigious Ecole Normale Supérieure, a teacher-training institute for secondary and higher education based in the heart of left-bank Paris, which attracted France's intellectual elite (Moi 1994: 49). In 1925, women were not permitted to study there and went instead to the women-only branch of the Ecole Normale Supérieure at Sèvres, in the south-west suburbs of Paris, where philosophy was not taught, or to the Sorbonne. Beauvoir's early philosophical study was nevertheless wide-ranging, encompassing thinkers as diverse as Plato (427–347 BC), Gottfried Leibniz (1646–1716), Immanuel Kant (1724–1804), Arthur Schopenhauer (1788–1860), Friedrich Nietzsche (1844–1900) and Henri-Louis Bergson (1859–1941), among others, as she developed her philosophical interests (Fullbrook 1998: 15–19).

During the 1920s, the thought of Georg Wilhelm Friedrich Hegel (1770–1831) and Karl Marx (1818–1883), who were later to prove important for Beauvoir, were not taught at the Sorbonne (*MDD*: 230). This can be explained by the narrowness of the Sorbonne philosophy curriculum at this time and by the rather marginalised existence of Hegelianism and Marxism until the 1930s in France. A Hegelian revival had begun in 1931 to mark the centenary of Hegel's death, which led to his major philosophical works appearing in French translation from 1939. Marx's socialist theories of history and society were little known in France before the 1880s and were then taken up by leading social-ists such as Jean Jaurès (1859–1914), who unified various group-ings into a socialist party, the Section Française de l'Internationale Socialiste (French Section of the Socialist International). However, after the First World War, the French socialist movement split into the Proudhonist socialists, led by Léon Blum (1872–1950), and the Communists or 'Parti Communiste Français' (French Communist Party), affiliated to the Moscow-based Third International (Soviet Communist Party). Marxism and the PCF then developed through the 1930s as a major political force in French society and influenced many writers and intellectuals, including Beauvoir, as we will see in Chapter 1. She was, however, exposed to certain ideas of Hegel and

Marx in the 1920s because she knew Marxist intellectuals, such as Paul Nizan (1905–1940), who was a very close friend of Sartre's, and Georges Politzer (1903–1942) (*MDD*: 236–237).

In 1929, Beauvoir formed a lifelong personal and intellectual partnership with Sartre. Having completed her training, Beauvoir worked as a philosophy teacher in secondary schools in Marseille, Rouen and Paris, then in 1943, on the publication of her first novel, *She Came to Stay*, she turned to a career as a full-time writer. Through the publication of their philosophy, novels and plays, Beauvoir and Sartre became the leading figures of French atheistic existentialism, one of the most influential literary, philosophical and artistic movements of the twentieth century. In 1945, they launched *Les Temps Modernes*, a left-wing, non-aligned political and literary review, which was highly influential in intellectual debates in the 1940s and 1950s. Overseas travel, especially contact with the US, was also crucial to Beauvoir's development as a thinker. The year 1947 saw her first visit to the US, which was to prove important for her research into women's lives for *The Second Sex*. During this visit, she wrote *America Day by Day* (1954) as a diary record of her journey and began a four-year relationship with the American social realist writer, Nelson Algren (1909–1981). Beauvoir's regular visits to the US enabled her to gain an awareness of the situation of women and of the black population. In 1949, her ground-breaking study of women's condition, *The Second Sex*, was published in France, the first volume selling 22,000 copies in the first week. She continued to publish fiction, winning the prestigious Goncourt Prize in 1954 for *The Mandarins*, a portrait of post-war intelligentsia in the grip of cold war ethical dilemmas. Although she broadly sympathised with Communism in the 1940s, it was only in the 1950s, during the Algerian War (1954–1962), that Beauvoir became directly and actively involved in politics, supporting the Algerian struggle for independence from France and openly condemning French government policy in North Africa. In the mid 1950s, she began working on *Memoirs of a Dutiful Daughter*, the first volume of her extensive memoirs, which were published in France in four volumes from 1958 until 1972 and subsequently were widely translated. Her memoirs have constituted a widely influential case study of a twentieth-century woman intellectual bearing witness to many of the major political and cultural events of the twentieth century as well as to her own intellectual trajectory as a writer and philosopher.

In 1965, in an interview with Francis Jeanson (Beauvoir 1966), she declared herself 'completely feminist', an important political statement given Beauvoir's major international status by the mid 1960s. Then, in the post-1968 period, Beauvoir found a new audience for *The Second Sex* among second-wave Anglo-American and French feminists. In 1968, a major upheaval had occurred in French society, which started as a student revolt against the French university system in Paris and, supported by the trade unions, became a wider political crisis in France with long-lasting consequences. These entailed the rise of the Parti Socialiste (Socialist Party) as the main left-wing party to the detriment of the Parti Communiste Français and the resignation in 1969 of the autocratic right-wing leader, General Charles de Gaulle (1890–1970) from the political stage, which he had dominated since the 1940s with his vision of strong French national identity and sovereignty.

The range of feminist debates and campaigns which took place over the centuries prior to 1968 had centred on female suffrage, birth control and women's emancipation more generally. After 1968, the 'Mouvement de libération des femmes', or MLF, rejected the reformist approach of this earlier 'first-wave' French feminism, giving rise to what is now known as 'post-1968' or 'second-wave' French feminism. The MLF resists easy definition as it comprised many different groupings. 'Psychanalyse et politique', for example, was a separatist group, led by Antoinette Fouque, which sought to overthrow patriarchy by revaluing feminine specificity or difference, partly through its theoretical engagement with Freudian psychoanalysis. Two other main groups, the 'class struggle tendency', or socialist feminists, and the 'radical feminists' took Marxism as their theoretical base, although they each adopted different approaches to women's liberation. The 'class struggle tendency' group sought to link women's oppression with social class oppression, fighting within the socialist movement. The 'radical feminists' rejected formal organisational structures and sought to combat the material oppression of women in patriarchal society by focusing on issues such as abortion and violence against women.

Beauvoir was actively involved in feminist campaigns, such as the fight to legalise abortion, and became editorial director of *Questions Féministes* (later *Nouvelles Questions Féministes*), an important feminist journal. In 1974 she also assumed the presidency of the 'Ligue des droits de la femme' (League for Women's Rights). Beauvoir was staunchly opposed to French 'differentialist' feminism associated with 'Psychanalyse et politique', preferring to lend her support to the radical materialist feminist tendency, centred around figures such as Christine Delphy (1941–) and Monique Wittig (1935–2003), both key activists and theorists of post-1968 French feminism. She campaigned actively in the 1970s on issues such as legalising abortion and raising awareness of violence against women.

Beauvoir's last major philosophical study, *Old Age*, was published in France in 1970. Then, after the death of Sartre in 1980, she published a tribute to her lifelong companion, *Adieux: A Farewell to Sartre* (1981). She died on 14 April 1986 and was buried with Sartre in Montparnasse cemetery in Paris. Since Beauvoir's death, her Second World War diary and letters to Nelson Algren and to Sartre have been published.

Beauvoir's extraordinary life and distinguished intellectual career were – as she was well aware – largely untypical of the majority of French women of the period. Yet she did not experience an unfettered path to such distinction. To engage with Beauvoir's thought entails a recognition of the complexities of intellectual women's lives in a traditionally patriarchal society and of the gender politics that structure intellectual enquiry and debate. In Beauvoir's case, the path she negotiated to distinction involved her self-construction as a literary writer rather than as a philosopher and her pursuit of an intellectual life with Sartre. Yet, until relatively recently, this meant that she tended to be perceived more as Sartre's disciple, rather than as a philosophical thinker possessing her own distinctive body of thought. As the feminist philosopher, Michèle Le Doeuff, has argued, this has much to do with women's position in philosophy more generally, and Simone de Beauvoir's situation in particular (Le Doeuff 1989). In recent years, however, there has been a surge of interest in Beauvoir's philosophy. This re-evaluation of her thought is embodied in the existence of this volume, which approaches her literary and philosophical writing as mutually complementary and infused with the same philosophical apprehension of the world. Nevertheless, Beauvoir did make a distinction between her philosophical writing, which reflected her 'practical choices and intellectual certitudes', and her fictional writing, which, informed by a different order of experience, explored the 'ambiguity' or irreducible indeterminacy of existence (*FC*: 332). In this way, as we will see in the subsequent chapters, although Beauvoir is engaged with similar problems on occasions in her philosophical and literary writing, her way of engaging with those problems varies according to the type of writing undertaken. For example, 'the problem of the Other' is explored in both her philosophical essay, *Pyrrhus et Cinéas* (1944) and her second novel, *The Blood of Others* (1945). However, in the former text, Beauvoir is concerned to define certain intellectual principles drawn from the particularity of concrete human experience, whereas, in the latter fictional context, she explores the ambiguity of the 'lived experience' of her characters on an imaginary plane, without providing any analysis of that experience. In short, her philosophical writing, informed by concrete experience, provides an intellectual analysis of experience, whereas her literary writing explores the ambiguity of that experience. With these distinctions in mind, this study – in the spirit of the series – will concentrate primarily on Beauvoir's thought as it is articulated in her main theoretical writings, with references to the theoretical preoccupations of her literary writing, informed as they are by her philosophical approach.

BEAUVOIR'S KEY IDEAS

The ensuing discussion is organised around various 'key ideas' already mentioned in this introduction. Chapter 1 explains the basic concepts of atheistic existentialism and phenomenology, which are crucial to an understanding of Beauvoir's subsequent thinking on ethics, gender and ageing. Existential phenomenology can be difficult for non-philosophers because – like any branch of thought – it is a synthesis of ideas already complex in themselves. Nevertheless, its emphasis on subjective, everyday 'lived experience' should help you orient yourself. This initial chapter shows how Beauvoir was influenced by several philosophers in her own distinctive development of existential phenomenology, including Hegel, the Danish philosopher, Søren Kierkegaard (1813–1855), and the German phenomenologists, Edmund Husserl (1859–1938) and Martin Heidegger (1889–1976). In the early 1940s, we will see that, although Beauvoir was working in the same philosophical context as Jean-Paul Sartre, her focus (as distinct from his) tends to be primarily ethical (concerned with how we live our lives) rather than ontological (concerned with the nature of being).

In Chapter 2, we begin to examine Beauvoir's philosophical writing. Reading *Pyrrhus et Cinéas* (1944), *The Ethics of Ambiguity* (1947) and her essays on the Marquis de Sade (1951–1952) and Brigitte Bardot, her attempt to develop an ethics based on existential phenomenology is assessed alongside her theorisation of an ethics of the erotic. In *Pyrrhus et Cinéas* and *The Ethics of Ambiguity*, Beauvoir introduces several key concepts, such as situation, reciprocity, ambiguity, disclosure and appeal, which inform her analyses of women's condition in *The Second Sex*.

Chapter 3 examines *The Second Sex* as a study of woman's subjectivity and oppression, which draws on existential phenomenology, Marxism and anthropology. Probing Beauvoir's influential and well-known assertion in *The Second Sex* that 'one is not born, but rather becomes, a woman', Chapter 3 analyses what 'becoming a woman' means in her account of the construction of female subjectivity in a traditionally patriarchal society and explores Beauvoir's similarly influential notion of woman as 'the absolute Other'.

Chapter 4 addresses the ways in which Beauvoir's feminist thinking developed after the publication of *The Second Sex* and during the post-1968 period, during which she became politically active in the French feminist movement. In the 1970s, she did not reject her original arguments in *The Second Sex* – although disillusioned with socialism, she now recognised that it would not incorporate a feminist revolution of society. She also acknowledged that she had underestimated the political significance of women's sexuality and she now recognised that, in all political struggles, theory should now be derived from collective political practice.

In Chapter 5, we consider Beauvoir's theory of literature, articulated in key statements from the mid 1940s until the early 1980s. Beauvoir's critical philosophical thinking informed her view of 'committed' or 'engagé' writing and the ways in which literature might explore the 'ambiguity' of singular lived experience. The chapter examines the formal implications of her notion of literature as necessarily 'committed' for her textual practice, particularly in the context of the representation of women's situation in her fictional writing. It also analyses Beauvoir's view of authentic literature for its ability to transcend the separation and alienation between human beings if it constitutes a genuine quest and communicative encounter between author and reader.

Chapter 6 concentrates on Beauvoir's study of ageing, *Old Age*, for its bid to elucidate how ageing affects the 'lived experience' of subjectivity. It is argued that there is no universal experience of ageing, which depends on the interaction of physiological, psychological, historical, geographical and socio-cultural variables. Old age, like gender in *The Second Sex*, is represented as a *cultural* not a natural fact.

The final chapter, 'After Beauvoir', sketches briefly the impact of her thought on second-wave feminism and highlights the continuing relevance of her thought. In the 'Further Reading' section, an annotated and comprehensive list of Beauvoir's own works is provided, followed by a list of interviews. The second part of this section suggests other studies of her work which might usefully be consulted as further reading to this present volume. Full details of all other works referenced in the text are provided in the 'Works Cited' section.

Readers new to Simone de Beauvoir's thought are at the beginning of an exciting intellectual journey; this volume aims to help them on their first step!

KEY IDEAS

1

EXISTENTIALISM

Simone de Beauvoir is often associated with the strand of atheistic existentialism which developed in France during the Second World War and found its expression in philosophical texts as well as in prose fiction, drama, music and the visual arts of the period. As well as providing part of the philosophical context for *The Second Sex* and *Old Age*, existentialism informs Beauvoir's literary practice. It is important, then, that we examine the basic notions associated with French atheistic existentialism before turning to other aspects of her work. This chapter also begins to explore Beauvoir's interpretation and ethical critique of existentialist philosophy.

Initially, Beauvoir claimed that she and Sartre did not understand what 'existentialism' meant! Commenting on the reception of her second novel, *The Blood of Others*, in 1945, Beauvoir writes in her autobiography:

> It was labelled not only a 'Resistance novel' but also an 'Existentialist novel'. Henceforth this label was to be affixed automatically to any work by Sartre or myself. [. . .] Sartre had refused to allow Gabriel Marcel to apply this adjective to him: 'My philosophy is a philosophy of existence; I don't even know what "Existentialism" is.' I shared his irritation. I had written my novel before I had even encountered the term 'Existentialist'; my inspiration came from my own experience, not from a system. But our protests were in vain. In the end, we took the epithet that everyone used for us and used it for our own purposes.

> (*FC*: 45–46)

EXISTENTIALISM

What is existentialism? The term is sometimes used narrowly in connection with the work of Jean-Paul Sartre; however, it refers more generally to the work of several nineteenth- and twentieth-century philosophers, such as Søren Kierkegaard (1813–1855), Friedrich Nietzsche (1844–1900), Karl Jaspers (1883–1969), Martin Heidegger (1889–1976), Gabriel Marcel (1889–1973), Jean-Paul Sartre (1905–1980), Maurice Merleau-Ponty (1908–1961) and Simone de Beauvoir. Most of these thinkers rejected the 'existentialist' label and preferred to describe their work as 'existential philosophy' or as 'a philosophy of existence'. If existentialism could be summarised in three words, they might be 'freedom', 'responsibility' and 'authenticity'. Existentialists claim that human beings have no predetermined purpose or essence laid down by God or nature. They are responsible for creating their lives according to their own values – and not by following the 'herd' – by reflecting clearly on their situation and relationships and by acting authentically.

The origins of existentialism can be traced far back into the history of philosophy in its rejection of essentialism or the notion that human beings have an inner nature or essence. However, French atheistic existentialism, as it is represented in Beauvoir's thought, is the result of a complex and partial synthesis of several philosophers' ideas, the first of these being Hegel. Indeed, modern existentialism originated in the nineteenth century as a reaction, initiated by Kierkegaard, to the abstract rationalism of Hegel's philosophy.

HEGEL

Hegel's philosophy was the central philosophical influence on the thought of the German Communist thinkers, Karl Marx (1818–1883) and Friedrich Engels (1820–1895) and has had a huge influence in philosophy, history and politics. Hegel was a German idealist philosopher who published four major works in his lifetime: *Phenomenology of Spirit* (1807), described by Marx as 'the true birthplace and secret of Hegel's philosophy'; *Science of Logic* (1812–1816); *Encyclopedia* (1817, 1827, 1830) and *Philosophy of Right* (1821), although, as we shall see, it was his *Phenomenology of Spirit* which had the greatest influence on Beauvoir's thought.

Hegel was interested in how we achieve knowledge of what we call 'reality'. He argued in *Phenomenology of Spirit* that this 'spirit', or self-consciousness, travels on its way through various stages of consciousness on its quest for absolute knowledge. This journey involves a fitful progression from error to enlightenment to greater self-knowledge – a bit of a metaphor for life really! Hegel viewed history as the realisation of this spirit of freedom, which proceeds through the three dialectical phases of thesis, antithesis and synthesis towards reason.

Judith Butler, a highly influential theorist in contemporary gender studies, has described Hegel's travelling self-consciousness as a cartoon figure, always encountering obstacles and difficulties and having to pick itself up, dust itself down and start again (Butler 1987: 21). What stops this spirit, or self-consciousness, abandoning its quest is desire – first, to overcome the obstacles encountered and, second, to achieve ultimate self-knowledge. But the spirit can only know itself through another self-consciousness, which will be sacrificed to the spirit's search. Indeed, Hegel thought that historical development or dialectical change can only occur through a confrontation between self-consciousnesses.

Unlike René Descartes (1596–1650), a founder of modern philosophy who, in his quest for the foundations of knowledge, presumed that a self-conscious, self-knowing subject (known as 'the cogito') was the source and guarantee of knowledge, Hegel argued in the *Phenomenology* that a self-consciousness cannot exist without the Other.

DIALECTIC

The term 'dialectic' refers to a philosophical process and is particularly associated with Hegel, although it has its roots in the works of the Ancient Greek philosopher, Plato. A dialectical movement involves asserting a thesis which is then negated by its antithesis and subsequently resolved in the synthesis, which in turn becomes the next thesis and so on. An example of dialectical thinking might be: Thesis: 'All dogs chase cats'; Anti-thesis: 'My dog, who lives in the same house as cats, does not chase cats'; Synthesis/New thesis: 'Some dogs chase cats'.

Hegel thus introduced the notion of 'alterity', or otherness, as the necessary condition for the existence of self-consciousness (Grosz 1989: 3). Each self-consciousness requires the recognition of the Other, then, to achieve self-certainty and this recognition is achieved through the process known as 'the master–slave dialectic'. This was one of the key concepts in Hegel's system and was especially important for Beauvoir and Sartre. It was also adopted and adapted by Marxism, existentialism and absorbed into much of post-1945 French thought.

THE MASTER–SLAVE DIALECTIC

The master–slave dialectic is a concept which appears in Hegel's *Phenomenology of Spirit*, in his account of self-consciousness (Hegel 1977: 111–119). Self-consciousness is the characteristic which distinguishes human beings from other things in the world. Note here that the German word for self-consciousness, 'Selbstbewusstsein', can also mean 'being self-assured', so it has a positive meaning (rather than the negative connotations of embarrassment associated with the English word, 'self-consciousness'). He argues that self-consciousness cannot exist in isolation, for it needs an external object – that is, another self-consciousness – from which it can differentiate itself. I can only be aware of myself if I am aware of something else which is not myself. But this external object, desired by self-consciousness as a means to define itself, is also a threat. Self-consciousness cannot negate or obliterate this external object because, in so doing, it will negate or obliterate the means of its own existence. To achieve confirmation of the certainty of its existence, self-consciousness needs to be recognised as such by another self-consciousness: human beings need to recognise each other as similarly conscious beings in the world to be sure that they exist. So being 'recognised' by another human being potentially enables the subject to gain reassurance of the fact of his/her own existence or ontological security, but such recognition can also constitute a threat. Why? When two people meet, they each seek a reflection of themselves in the other. In so doing, one person is objectified or rendered an Other who is then experienced as a threat to the subject. Each self-consciousness tries to display itself as pure 'being-for-itself', or pure existence, with no attachment to vulnerable material objects, such as its own body or the body of the Other. A struggle for life or death is embarked upon to demonstrate this lack of attachment to materiality and thus to prove his/her active universality. So the initial mode of engagement between these two self-consciousnesses is not recognition of each other, but conflict, caused by existential fear and need (for recognition). This conflict between self and Other cannot, of course, end in death because such an outcome would destroy all possibility of recognition. So one person gives way, thereby negating his/her independence and positioning him/herself as the 'slave' to the independent 'master'. But the master, despite enjoying the fruits of the slave's labour, does not receive the independent recognition s/he sought from a 'free' being because the slave is bound to the material world with no independent consciousness. However, all is not lost for the slave for s/he mediates the master's relationship with the material world. Through this direct connection with the material world, the slave gains a certain satisfaction through his/her labours and consciousness of him/herself and of his/her oppression. The slave therefore objectifies or externalises him/herself through his/her labour and it is this ability to change the material world through his/her own efforts and the slave's fear of death which will ultimately lead to his/her freedom. The master, however, remains condemned to enjoy the fruits of domination while becoming more and more detached from the world, deprived of the recognition that s/he initially sought. The 'journey' of the spirit and its passage through the master–slave dialectic is, of course, not to be understood literally! But Hegel's account of the journey of 'spirit' describes how subjects or individuals come into being and how they are mutually dependent on each other and their labour in the world for a sense of selfhood. This account can be exemplified in personal and collective relationships – how people, local communities and nation states might recognise that respectful cooperation and mutual 'give and take' tends to work better as a model for diplomatic self–Other interaction than attempting to impose one's will and personal desires violently upon others, which tends to lead ultimately to rejection, isolation and possibly, annihilation.

NEO-HEGELIANISM

Neither Beauvoir nor Sartre studied Hegel in depth before 1940. Prior to the 1930s, there was little interest in Hegel in France, partly due to the dominance of the Cartesian and Kantian philosophical traditions

(Lundgren-Gothlin 1996: 56). As noted in Chapter 1, Beauvoir trained as a philosopher in the 1920s and was not exposed to the philosophies of Hegel, Husserl or Heidegger at the Sorbonne; yet these philosophers were to prove influential in her later thought. She became acquainted with these thinkers in the 1930s, when a certain synthesis between the ideas of Kierkegaard and the phenomenology of Husserl and Heidegger was encouraged because existentialism and phenomenology (the study of how things appear to consciousness) were both introduced

KARL MARX (1818–1883)

Karl Marx was a left-wing political philosopher whose analyses of 'capitalism' have proved enormously influential across the world in the twentieth century, although his theories have borne little relation to the political regimes and ideologies which claim to be 'Marxist'. Marx's revolutionary philosophy is, importantly, based on a *materialist* analysis of society; in other words, an analysis which focuses on the concrete world in which people live and the ways in which social structures and everyday practices contribute to its being an inequitable and oppressive place. Marx focused on the economic organisation of society (the 'base') and argued that all aspects of life were, ultimately, explicable through underlying economic relations. Out of the economic 'base' grows the 'superstructure' (comprising, for example, law, political representation, religion and culture) which sustains that 'base'. Human behaviour could be explained by the ways in which different social classes have competed against each other for money or for the means of wealth production. Drawing on Hegel's account of the master–slave dialectic and of history as a dialectical process, Marx developed ideas such as the theory of 'alienated labour', whereby the worker loses the object of his/her labour to his/her employer who, in profiting from this labour, makes more capital and gains more power over the worker. The solution to such inequities, for Marx, was the abolition of private property and of oppression. The influence of Marx's thought on existential phenomenology can be seen in the latter's emphasis on labour as a fundamental human activity and on the pairing of Hegel's master–slave dialectic with Marx's idea of class struggle (Lundgren-Gothlin 1996: 85). In *The Second Sex*, as we will see in Chapter 3, Beauvoir uses various Marxist ideas, such as 'alienation' and the importance of productive activity for human development and history.

to France at approximately the same time (Lundgren-Gothlin 1996: 133). Furthermore, phenomenology became more widely known at approximately the same time as a revival of interest in Hegel's *Phenomenology of Spirit*, stimulated by Alexandre Kojève and Jean Hyppolite who respectively provided existentialist and Marxist interpretations of the text. This neo-Hegelian revival, led by Kojève and Hyppolite, inspired a new generation of French thinkers – including Beauvoir and Sartre – to discover Hegel's *Phenomenology of Spirit* and other writings. Hegel's philosophy would acquire a new, radical interpretation, which drew on Marxist theory and existential phenomenology.

Kojève's seminars on Hegel, which took place in Paris between 1933 and 1939, were highly influential and attended by figures such as the sociologist, Raymond Aron (1905–1983), the philosopher, Maurice Merleau-Ponty (1908–1961), who later worked with Sartre and Beauvoir at *Les Temps Modernes*, and the Freudian revisionist psychoanalyst, Jacques Lacan (1901–1981). All later went on to become major figures in post-war French thought. Simone de Beauvoir probably did not attend these seminars; however, she read Kojève's work on Hegel and was a close friend of Merleau-Ponty at this time. In this way, Beauvoir's interpretation of Hegel was most probably influenced by these Marxist and existentialist readings of *Phenomenology of Spirit*.

The importance of this neo-Hegelian revival for Beauvoir and her generation was that Kojève placed the question of subjectivity and self-consciousness and the relationship with the Other at the heart of politics and history (Grosz 1989: 5–6). Kojève emphasised the dialectical nature of history as it is produced through struggle and resistance. Subjectivity and self-knowledge were not conceptualised as isolated from the other and the world as in the Cartesian system, but as a product of the self-conscious subject's encounters with the Other, the community and its institutions.

As we will see in more detail in Chapter 3, like Kojève, Beauvoir was especially interested in Hegel's master–slave dialectic, using a quotation from his *Phenomenology* as the epigraph ('each consciousness seeks the death of the other') to her first novel, *She Came to Stay* – unfortunately omitted in the English translation of the novel.

In *The Second Sex*, Beauvoir adapts the master–slave dialectic to the relationship between men and women in patriarchal society. However, her reading of Hegel is influenced by Kojève's existentialist reading,

SHE CAME TO STAY, 1943

Beauvoir's first published novel, *She Came to Stay* (*L'Invitée*) (1943) is a fictionalised account of a trio relationship between Beauvoir, Sartre and Olga Kosakievicz. Set in Paris in the late 1930s among the theatre circle, the action centres on the triangular relationship between Françoise Miquel, Pierre Labrousse and Xavière Pagès, a young provincial woman from Rouen, and the ethical problems posed thereby. Dealing with the concrete threat posed by a third party ('the problem of the Other' in existentialist terms) to an established heterosexual relationship, Beauvoir's novel is a dense evocation of sexual and moral dilemmas in existentialist Paris. Infused with key existentialist concepts such as 'nothingness', 'being-for-itself', being-in-itself', 'recognition' and 'the look of the Other' (for further explanation, see pp. 26–27), *She Came to Stay* is an excellent illustration of concepts and themes associated with existential phenomenology.

in which Hegel's 'geist' or 'spirit' is replaced by 'man' and God is replaced by 'the end of history'. In Beauvoir's appropriation of Hegel, there is no reconciliation between subject and object, spirit and self-consciousness (Mackenzie in Evans 1998: 128). We have to assume the ambiguities of our situation by attempting to live an ethical life. Kojève reads the master–slave dialectic as driven by the desire to be and for recognition, which will culminate in the slave's emancipation through labour. The slave will therefore transcend the given and create history which, for Kojève, is a story of the battle between masters and slaves (Lundgren-Gothlin 1996: 64). For Kojève, as for Beauvoir, as we will see in Chapter 3, the struggle between master and slave, man and woman is, crucially, an historical one and, hence, subject to change. In this way, her notion of 'becoming woman' draws on the Hegelian notion of subjectivity as *dialectical* – a subject-in-process. She also emphasises, like Kojève, the possibility of reciprocal recognition between master and slave, man and woman, as a solution to the struggle for recognition which is fundamental to and recurrent in history (Lundgren-Gothlin 1996: 70–71). Hegel's notion of intersubjective recognition enables Beauvoir to dispense with Descartes's notion that self-consciousness occurs *within* the cogito (Mackenzie in Evans 1998: 127). For Beauvoir, as for Hegel, self-consciousness is a result of the self–Other relation. In other words, we need other people to become ourselves.

KIERKEGAARD

Against the abstract rationalism and universalism of Hegel's 'spirit', Kierkegaard emphasised the irreducibility of the subjective experience of the individual. He described this as the point of view of the 'existing individual'. This distinctive use of the word 'existence' to mean a specifically human mode of being led to the term 'existentialism' (from the Danish and German word, '*existenz*') being coined in the twentieth century by the French Catholic existentialist, Gabriel Marcel (1889– 1973). Kierkegaard rejected what he saw as Hegel's attempt to put the human subject in the place of God; instead, he defended the partial, limited and subjective viewpoint from which human judgements and choices are made. Everyday life, he thought, was essentially experienced at a subjective level; each individual experiences her/his own reality, not an objective reality. For this reason, he was opposed to abstract philosophical systems. According to Kierkegaard, each individual is free to choose a way of life, but this freedom is also a cause of 'angst' (anguish) because it constitutes a great responsibility. S/he can choose to live inauthentically, for example, by pursuing self-gratification in the moment, or authentically, for example, by living an ethical life. Anguish is eradicated by a 'leap' into religious faith. Freedom is thus the freedom to choose God (Lundgren-Gothlin 1996: 129).

Simone de Beauvoir refers to her understanding of the conflict between the Hegelian and Kierkegaardian viewpoints in *The Prime of Life*. Reading Hegel and rereading Kierkegaard in 1940, she saw their respective philosophies as a temptation between submerging one's individual self into Hegel's 'universal being' and attributing significance to the existence and presence of Kierkegaard's individual – in short, a confrontation between the universal and the particular perspectives. Despite her admiration for aspects of Hegel's system, Beauvoir welcomed Kierkegaard's defence of 'the living certainty of "I am, I exist, here and now, I am myself"' and recognised – in the midst of the Second World War – that 'no individual can lose himself in the circumambient universe' (*PL*: 469–470). Existentialism's emphasis on freedom, choice, responsibility and anguish came from Kierkegaard, although Beauvoir and Sartre transposed these elements into a secular context, for they were both atheists; additionally, they were influenced by German phenomenology (see section below).

Briefly, here, we should note in passing the general influence of Nietzsche on the development of atheistic existentialism, although his specific influence on the development of Beauvoir's thought is relatively minor. At this general level, Nietzsche's rejection of God and his notion of the human subject as being driven by the 'will to power' in a universe in which there can be no universal moral laws find broad echoes in existentialism. Beauvoir shares with Nietzsche a similar concern for freedom, power and authenticity, but her work lacks the nihilism (the contention that nothing is of any value or even exists) and bleak view of human relations and morality found in his work (Lundgren-Gothlin 1996: 226).

In addition to Hegel, Kierkegaard and Nietzsche, the philosophies of Edmund Husserl and Martin Heidegger – in the shape of phenomenology – played a major role in what has come to be known as French atheistic existentialism.

HUSSERL AND PHENOMENOLOGY

Husserl is usually viewed as the founder of phenomenology, a branch of philosophy whose aim is to study how external things – or, in other words, objects of consciousness, such as natural phenomena in the world, other people, our thoughts and feelings – 'appear' to human consciousness. By a process of suspending or 'bracketing off' our assumptions about the status of the existence of these 'appearances' (known as 'the phenomenological reduction', or epoché), we are able to perceive the pure phenomena of the things 'in themselves' or the objects of consciousness as we experience them.

Husserl wanted to make philosophy more rigorous in its methods; his approach is 'epistemological' (from the Greek 'episteme' meaning 'knowledge') in that he wanted to analyse the basis of knowledge or question how we know what we know. Phenomenology is concerned, then, with analysing the perceptual interaction between people (or consciousnesses) and the world. It focuses especially on how we know what we know about the world through analysing our respective lived experiences of the world. Phenomenology views all knowledge of the world as 'situated', or relative to the perceiving consciousness and context of the given moment.

One of the truths revealed by the phenomenological method, according to Husserl, is that consciousness is intentional. This means that consciousness is always directed towards something or is of something. In this way, Husserl differentiates between acts of consciousness and objects of consciousness. When I am conscious of something, such as a book on the shelf or that I love my dog, a collection of sense data and experience are unified in an act of intentional consciousness relating to the book or the dog. But that act of consciousness is distinct from the object of consciousness (the book or the dog) which consciousness is directed to or 'intends'. In developing a phenomenological method, Husserl's aim was to expose the presuppositions and structures of experience and to discover an absolute foundation for knowledge in the shape of the transcendental ego or impersonal consciousness.

For Beauvoir and Sartre, the big attraction of phenomenology was that it was a philosophical method which focused on actual lived experience. Introduced to phenomenology by Raymond Aron, Beauvoir relates in *The Prime of Life* how Sartre saw it as a means for philosophy to describe the perceptual experiences of everyday life:

> Here was just the thing he had been longing to achieve for years – to describe objects just as he saw and touched them, and extract philosophy from the process. Aron convinced him that phenomenology fitted in with his special preoccupations: by-passing the antithesis of idealism and realism, affirming simultaneously both the supremacy of reason and the reality of the visible world as it appears to our senses.
>
> (*PL*: 135)

However, Sartre, in his own existential phenomenology (sketched out on pp. 25–27), would reject or revise certain Husserlian concepts such as the 'phenomenological reduction', or 'epoché', and 'transcendental ego'. In fact, it was to Martin Heidegger's development of Husserlian phenomenology that both Beauvoir and Sartre would turn, retaining nevertheless certain Husserlian notions in their respective interpretations of existential phenomenology (Cooper 1999: 46–47). The first of these is the importance accorded to the 'Lebenswelt' or the 'life-world' of perception and praxis (or practical action on the world with a view to transforming it in some way). The second debt to Husserl was his rejection of the Cartesian cogito as 'thinking substance' being causally related to other substances in the world. Lastly, Husserl's notion of the 'intentionality' of consciousness – or that consciousness is 'directed towards' objects and that it bestows meanings on those objects – is fundamental to existentialism.

HEIDEGGER

One of the reasons for Beauvoir and Sartre's greater interest in Heidegger's phenomenology was his interest in ontology or the science of being (from the Greek '*on, ontos*', meaning 'being'). Heidegger had been a student of Husserl's in Freiburg and is considered by some to be the 'first true Existentialist' (Warnock 1970: 46), although he rejected that description of his work and dissociated himself from what he saw as Sartre's 'humanistic' existentialism. Heidegger's most well-known work is perhaps *Being and Time* (*Sein und Zeit*), first published in 1927. As this title suggests, Heidegger was concerned with the meaning of being, particularly human being or, as he termed it, '*Dasein*' ('being-there'). He rejected Husserl's phenomenological reduction and attempt to isolate the 'transcendental Ego' from the world. Instead, he viewed human beings as '*Dasein*' or 'thrown-into-the-world'. What counts, he thought, is that we are *here*, immersed in the world, not abstractly contemplating it from afar. The essence of '*Dasein*' is its existence and that essence is not made up of particular properties, but rather by different ways of 'being-in-the-world'. This is similar to Sartre's later claim in *Existentialism and Humanism* (1946) that 'existence precedes essence', which we will examine on p. 26. Furthermore, '*Dasein*' is 'ek-static' (from the Greek, '*ek-stasis*', or 'standing out from'), meaning that it is radically separated from itself by the three ecstases of past, present and future. So we can never 'just exist' in the present moment because the past, present and future are deeply enmeshed in our decisions to act.

According to Heidegger, human beings are also not alone in the world, but '*Mitsein*', or 'being-with-others'. Other people form part of our 'being-in-the-world', or 'thrown-ness', as do our locations in time and place. Heidegger sees '*Dasein*' as only truly authentic in its 'being-towards-death' because acceptance of our own mortality entails that we each accept that we are finite beings. '*Dasein*' is individualised by death, since no one else can experience my death for me. Heidegger described this proper acceptance of one's death as '*Eigentlichkeit*', which came to be translated by French existentialists as 'authenticity'. In this way, he saw the authentic positioning of '*Dasein*' in relation to death as the means through which 'temporality' (or the human subject's experience of time) and time itself form the basis of the meaning of being.

SARTRE

In addition to Beauvoir, Sartre is the other figure usually associated with French existentialism and his work has had a major influence on subsequent thinkers in the post-war period. He occupied a key role in relation to Simone de Beauvoir as her primary intellectual interlocutor, as well as her lifelong partner. No account of the development of Beauvoir's thought would be complete without some discussion of Sartrean existentialism and the ways in which Beauvoir and Sartre influenced each other's work.

We have already noted that Beauvoir and Sartre shared a strong interest in phenomenology, which began in the early 1930s. In one of his earliest philosophical texts, *The Transcendence of the Ego* (1936), Sartre rejects Husserl's claim that there is a 'transcendental ego' or a residual 'self' that is a necessary condition for our experience. Instead, Sartre argues that there is a unity of consciousness and that it is free. So there cannot be a separate part of consciousness that directs the rest of consciousness; consciousness cannot simultaneously act as subject and object for itself. Sartre also distinguishes here between reflexive and pre-reflexive consciousness. Reflexive consciousness is consciousness of consciousness, or the process whereby we are aware of being conscious. Pre-reflexive consciousness is the everyday awareness that we have of objects in the world. Sartre developed this notion of existential selfhood further in his main philosophical work on the subject, *Being and Nothingness*, published in 1943.

Being and Nothingness is subtitled 'An essay on phenomenological ontology' and is divided into four main sections dealing with 'nothingness', 'being-for-itself', 'being-for-others' and 'having, doing and being'. Like Beauvoir's *The Second Sex*, it is a complex work which draws on a range of philosophical approaches in its attempt to account for how human beings become conscious of their existence. In the first section, Sartre explains how there is a nothingness at the core of human reality; only human beings have the power to negate imaginatively their surroundings: 'consciousness is a being, the nature of which is to be conscious of the nothingness of its being' (BN: 47). This power to negate entails that, for Sartrean existentialism, human beings are free to determine themselves; there is no divine being that is responsible for directing their lives. Human beings have no nature or essence. We are constantly free to choose how we live, but not free not to choose. For not to choose how to live is still to choose not to choose! However, anguish results from this apprehension of 'nothingness' and of the necessity to 'make oneself' and therein lies the temptation of 'bad faith' and 'inauthenticity'.

BAD FAITH

'Bad faith' is an important existentialist notion that refers to the ways in which human beings deceive themselves in order to pretend that they are not free. They are able to do this because human beings are both 'transcendent', because they 'go beyond' the given situation, and also a 'facticity', or bound to that given situation by their bodies, their past and other elements that are not chosen. So being 'in bad faith' means that we try to pretend that we are not free and that we are part of the inert given situation, while at the same time being aware that we are transcendent beings and could choose to change the situation – but our anguish at the realisation of our freedom prevents us from doing so. In *Being and Nothingness*, Sartre gives the example of a waiter in a Paris café who pretends to be no more than a waiter in a café. The waiter behaves as if to serve customers were the essence of his being, when in fact he is able to reflect on and transcend his situation (BN: 59–60).

In *Being and Nothingness*, Sartre distinguishes between various types of being: 'being-for-itself', the active existing of a free, conscious individual; 'being-in-itself', or the passive existing of inert non-human reality (for example, a stone); and 'being-for-others', or the way in which we exist as objects of other people's consciousnesses. In the second part of *Being and Nothingness*, Sartre examines the being of individual consciousness. Drawing on his earlier work in *The Transcendence of the Ego* and essays on the emotions and imagination, Sartre describes the isolation of consciousness, condemned to be free and always separated from coinciding with itself by the act of reflection, by its experience of being separated across time and by its 'being-for-others'.

The fact that we exist as objects for other people's consciousness is the main focus of the third section of Sartre's study. Here he examines how the existence of the Other is evident to us through 'the look' and through our various relationships of love, masochism, indifference, desire, hatred and sadism. Crucially, our realisation that the Other is a similarly free being like us leads us into perpetual conflict with the Other in a futile bid to achieve mastery over the meaning of the Other's gaze. Self–Other relationships in *Being and Nothingness* – based upon the Hegelian struggle between master and slave – are a gloomy affair, condemned to conflict. Yet the relationship with the Other is essential because it grounds our continuing attempts to construct an identity or 'essence'. In the final section of his study, Sartre explores how we are responsible for the way the world appears to us: we create the meaning of our lives. Freedom is a constant struggle and responsibility, assumed at an individual level, but also within a collective context.

Sartre finished *Being and Nothingness* indicating that he would publish a future work on ethics to complement his 1943 text. However, this unfinished work, *Notebooks for an Ethics*, was only published posthumously in 1983. It was Beauvoir who published the only existentialist ethics, entitled *The Ethics of Ambiguity*, in 1947. Indeed, a significant difference between Beauvoir's and Sartre's philosophical interests in the 1940s is that Beauvoir is concerned with ethics – how we should live our lives – and Sartre, as we have seen above, is concerned with phenomenology and ontology.

Another important point to note is that, although Beauvoir broadly shares with Sartre the same philosophical reference points, such as Hegel, Husserl, Heidegger and Kierkegaard, she often interprets these thinkers differently. This is less apparent in *Pyrrhus et Cinéas*, Beauvoir's first important philosophical essay, published in 1944, but becomes more apparent in *The Ethics of Ambiguity* and *The Second Sex*, which we will look at in Chapters 2 and 3.

SUMMARY

Simone de Beauvoir was influenced by several philosophers on her path to developing her own contribution to French existential phenomenology. From Kojève's reading of Hegel, she took an historical and existential interpretation of the master–slave dialectic. From Kierkegaard, she retained the notion of the existing individual in pursuit of an authentic, ethical life, but transposed to a secular context. Husserl's focus on consciousness's lived experience of the 'life-world' of perception and praxis would also be influential. Heidegger's notion of the human subject as being *'Dasein'* ('thrown-into-the-world'), *'Mitsein'* ('being-with-others'), and as 'being-towards-death' would also inform her ethics and account of gendered subjectivity in *The Second Sex*. Working in the same philosophical context as Sartre in the 1940s, her focus is primarily ethical rather than ontological.

2

ETHICS

To appreciate the distinctiveness of Beauvoir's contribution to existential phenomenology, and to prepare the philosophical ground for our study of *The Second Sex*, in this chapter we consider her two philosophical essays published in the 1940s: *Pyrrhus et Cinéas* (1944) (currently being translated) and *The Ethics of Ambiguity* (1947). We will also look briefly at two essays, written in the 1950s, in which Beauvoir explores the relationship between the ethical and the erotic, 'Must we burn Sade?' (1951–1952) and 'Brigitte Bardot and the Lolita syndrome' (1959).

In early 1943, Beauvoir was introduced to the term 'existentialism' and to Jean Grenier, a philosophy teacher and acquaintance of Sartre, who commissioned her to write *Pyrrhus et Cinéas* in the Café de Flore in Paris, later to be known as one of several hotbeds of existentialist debate:

> Grenier turned to me. 'What about you, madame?' he inquired. 'Are you an existentialist?' I can still recall my embarrassment at this question. I had read Kierkegaard, and the term 'existential philosophy' had been in circulation for some time apropos of Heidegger; but I didn't understand the meaning of the word 'existentialist', which Gabriel Marcel had recently coined.
>
> (*PL*: 547–548)

Beauvoir agreed to write what became *Pyrrhus et Cinéas*, which provides in part an ethical critique of Sartre's ideas in *Being and Nothingness*. She draws on the sources of existential phenomenology which we looked at in Chapter 1, such as Hegel, Heidegger, Husserl and Kierkegaard, and signals her disagreement with certain Sartrean notions of freedom, situation and intersubjective relations. It is Beauvoir's original interpretation of these notions that will be the focus of our discussion here. As we noted at the end of Chapter 1, although Beauvoir and Sartre are working broadly within the same philosophical framework in the 1940s, there are some important differences of interpretation between them.

SITUATION AND FACTICITY

'Situation' is a key concept in Beauvoir's thought and needs to be understood as a philosophical term rather than in its more familiar sense of 'context'. In Beauvoir's thought, 'situation' refers to how a human being as an individual consciousness is engaged in the world with regard to other people, to time, to space and to other products of his/her facticity. My 'situation' is not something outside or around me, but the glue which binds my freedom and my facticity together. 'Facticity' refers to the necessary connection between consciousness and the world of inert matter and the past. Aspects of my facticity are aspects of my situation which I have not chosen – for example, the facts of my birth, my body, the existence of other people, my death – and that I cannot choose not to accept as part of my situation. A non-situated consciousness is, by definition, impossible. The feminist theorist, Toril Moi, explains that the concept of 'situation' enables Beauvoir to avoid having to divide lived experience up into the traditional subject/object binary – precisely because the Other, for instance (as an example of my facticity) is always already part of that situation (Moi 1999: 65). Beauvoir's notion of the body as a situation is, according to Moi, a crucially original and often overlooked contribution to feminist theory (Moi 1999: 59).

In *Pyrrhus et Cinéas*, Beauvoir adopts the point of departure of the existing individual. Her focus, unlike Sartre in *Being and Nothingness*, is predominantly ethical rather than ontological, as she sets out to examine the importance of 'situation'.

One obvious difference between *Pyrrhus et Cinéas* and Sartre's *Being and Nothingness* and *Existentialism and Humanism* is one of tone – Beauvoir's essay is more optimistic and lacks the trenchant atheism and bleakness of Sartre's texts. Beauvoir does, however, broadly address the same existentialist topics, such as transcendence, action, freedom, the project and the role of the Other.

Pyrrhus et Cinéas is divided into two main sections: the first dealing with the features of individual human existence and the second examining the individual's relationship with other people. Beauvoir's initial focus – as indicated in a conversation between Pyrrhus (318–272 BC), the King of Epirus in Ancient Greece, and Cinéas, his adviser – is the contingency and consequent absurdity of human action: what is the point of action when there is always something else to be done? Beauvoir says that Cinéas's argument concerning the absurdity of human action is not the point; the point is that human beings are transcendent beings, oriented towards things beyond themselves and compelled to transcend the given. In this context, what is important is to create a meaningful existence in a meaningful world.

TRANSCENDENCE

'Transcendence' is a key term in existential phenomenology and refers to the process whereby human beings are compelled to go beyond a given state of affairs to pursue a further project (see Barnes's glossary in *BN*: 634; Fullbrook and Fullbrook 1998: 168). For example, once you have read this book, you might read all of Beauvoir's work and become a specialist in the area! In that way, you will have 'transcended' the given state of your knowledge by pursuing a project.

As transcendent beings, we can never exist or be fixed in the moment; here, Beauvoir takes up Heidegger's notion that 'Man is a creature of distances, he is always somewhere else'. What this means is that we are never entirely 'there', fixed in the moment, but always somehow engaged in transcending the given state of affairs. There is no privileged position from which we can have absolute knowledge of ourselves or other people because we are not fixed beings. For example, you might be sitting in a lecture taking notes, but you might also be thinking about the wonderful person you met the night before and planning a possible future with him/her, whether you need to go shopping on the way home, what you will be doing when you leave university, whether your dog recognises itself in the mirror and so on. In short, despite your best efforts of concentration, you can never be fully there in that moment because our capacity to transcend the given is hard-wired into our consciousness. Transcendence is simply part of the human condition. We are thus alien, or other, to ourselves and perpetually engaged in transcending the given situation as we construct ourselves. In so doing, we perpetually need to make choices, for to refuse to choose is to annihilate oneself.

In *Pyrrhus et Cinéas* Beauvoir refers to subjectivity as *intentional* consciousness (a notion derived from Brentano and Husserl, as we saw in Chapter 1, meaning that consciousness is always directed towards or of something). Like Sartre, she also uses the term 'transcendence' – although it will assume a different meaning because of the importance placed on the ethical implications of the existence of the Other in Beauvoir's philosophy. It is worth noting here that in *Being and Nothingness*, Sartre uses the term 'transcendence' (also derived from Husserlian phenomenology) sometimes as a synonym for 'the for-itself' and sometimes to indicate a process of being. In both cases consciousness moves towards the realisation of its own possibilities *by means of* the Other. Sartre acknowledges in *Being and Nothingness* that we exist in a world of others, but he maps consciousness's relation with the Other on to the Hegelian master–slave dialectic, representing it as a battle for supremacy:

> While I attempt to free myself from the hold of the Other, the Other is trying to free himself from mine; while I seek to enslave the Other, the Other seeks to enslave me. [. . .] The following descriptions of concrete behaviour [with others] must therefore be envisaged within the perspective of conflict. Conflict is the original meaning of being-for-others.
>
> (*BN*: 364)

Beauvoir, however, as we will see on pp. 34–36, emphasises the positive aspects of the self–Other relation. That does not mean that she does not recognise the potential for conflict in human relations, such as the occasional need for recourse to violence, but she is more interested in the possibilities of cooperation and solidarity which exist between people. Before looking at this area in more detail in *Pyrrhus et*

Cinéas, Beauvoir's analysis of death bears consideration, as it is a predominant theme in her work.

DEATH

In a section on 'the situation' at the end of Part I of *Pyrrhus et Cinéas*, Beauvoir discusses the role of death and the limits it might place on our projects. She concludes that death only puts an end to my projects once I am dead and rejects Heidegger's notion of the human being as a 'being-towards-death' (see Chapter 1, pp. 24–25). According to Beauvoir, to be human is to be mortal, so we cannot *choose* death, as it is part of our facticity; similarly, she refutes the notion that we exist for death. Unlike Heidegger, she does not accept that we live authentically only when we recognise that we are 'beings-towards-death'. Instead, 'being' as such has no end; only our projects can direct our existence towards a particular aim.

ALL MEN ARE MORTAL (1946)

In Beauvoir's third novel, *All Men are Mortal*, through the character of Fosca, Beauvoir explores the necessity of mortality and the fallacy of the Hegelian universal point of view in *Phenomenology of Spirit* (see Chapter 1, this volume). Like Virginia Woolf's *Orlando* (1928), the central character is immortal and seeks to extend his power to act across several centuries. A contemporary example of this refusal of mortality might be people who seek to have their bodies frozen when they die in the hope of benefiting at some future date from a cure for the disease which killed them and thereby artificially extending their lifespan. Fosca, however, becomes increasingly disillusioned with immortality and realises that it is precisely the finite nature of life which gives it value and that he must act collaboratively *with* others rather than arrogantly supposing he can act *for* them.

OTHER PEOPLE

As existing alone is impossible and undesirable as far as pursuing our projects are concerned, Beauvoir then asks what we can expect from other people who are indisputably in the world with us. In Part II, she explores various modes of relating to other people, such as self-sacrifice and ways in which individuals act for each other. She cites the example of the slave who obeys his/her master and the woman who sacrifices her life to her husband, stating that we can never abdicate our freedom – we simply conceal our freedom from ourselves by pretending that we are not free. Self-sacrifice is a way of existing 'for-others' and is also explored in the context of gender in *The Second Sex* (see, for example, the chapter on 'The woman in love' in the second volume) and in Beauvoir's fiction, notably in *The Mandarins* (1954) and *The Woman Destroyed*. In her discussion of self-sacrifice in *Pyrrhus et Cinéas*, Beauvoir examines the 'bad faith' which is involved in attempting to exist for the Other, and in mistakenly viewing oneself as the means to the Other's self-fulfilment. However, it is crucial to note here that she does not adopt the voluntaristic notion of freedom of Sartre's *Being and Nothingness*, which depends on a will to be free, effectively arguing that our actions are the product of 'free' choices. Instead, Beauvoir distinguishes between one's freedom and one's relative capacity to act in a given context. For Beauvoir, 'man is both freedom and facticity [. . .] he is free in situation' (*PC*: 326). These issues connected to freedom and the possibilities of action for one-self and for others would be developed in *The Ethics of Ambiguity* (see pp. 39–42) and in the context of gender relations in *The Second Sex* (see Chapter 3).

Beauvoir argues instead for a notion of the Other as potentially reciprocally equal – as a being who is always already included in this movement of consciousness towards its own perpetual self-construction. She argues that self–Other relations constitute recipro-cally the facticity of my situation or the given features of my existence in the world which I have not chosen. So the Other assumes the same

RECIPROCITY

Reciprocity is an important feature of self–Other relations for Beauvoir. It refers to a mode of relating to oneself and to others as both subject and object and as equal freedoms in the world. The importance that Beauvoir attributes to the moment of Hegelian recognition in the master–slave dialectic means that she emphasises the potential for reciprocity in our relation to the Other.

importance for me as other elements of my facticity, such as my body, my past and my birth. I did not choose these features of my existence and cannot choose to exist without them, although I can choose *how* to live them. So, for Beauvoir, we cannot alienate ourselves in the Other or retreat to being part of a collective identity to avoid the burden of individual responsibility for our existence. Existentially, the Other cannot be avoided! She or he represents a given feature of the individual's situation. Beauvoir explains that my individual freedom is always enmeshed with another's freedom, so that the limit of my freedom is the beginning of another's freedom. Freedom is therefore a collective responsibility.

Beauvoir contends that, although each person's experience of subjectivity is unique to him- or herself and that we each need to be 'recognised' for our unique individuality, we also need other people to be free beings – and that involves them acting as free subjects – in order to escape the 'contingency' or accidental fact of our existence. Indeed, it makes little sense, in Beauvoir's eyes, for one person to be free unless she or he acknowledges that other people are free, too:

> All men are free, and as soon as we have anything to do with other people, we experience their freedom. If we want to disregard these dangerous free beings, we have to turn away from mankind, but at that moment our being contracts and dwindles away. Our being can only be realised by choosing to risk itself in the world, by placing itself in danger of being grasped by other alien and divided free beings.

(*PC*: 349)

So, if we do not accept other people's freedom, we are then existentially diminished by the state of tyranny which ensues. As we will see in the context of oppressive gender relations in *The Second Sex*, this damages both parties involved. Other people's recognition of our existence and achievements in the world must be *freely* given rather than coerced. Beauvoir focuses, then, less on the conflictual aspects of relationships with others, and more on the potential for reciprocally free relations between self and Other.

An important concept in her discussion of relationships with other people is that of 'appeal', which Beauvoir introduces in *Pyrrhus et Cinéas* to mean an authentic mode of connection between human beings. Appealing to other people is a way of establishing a relationship between two transcendent human beings which respects their individual subjectivity while simultaneously bridging the distance between them. As Gothlin (1999: 90) notes, Sartre also uses the term 'appeal', but in two different ways: in *Being and Nothingness*, it is associated with the feminine and the obscene, whereas in the posthumously published *Notebooks for an Ethics* (1983), it is used to refer to an authentic connection between human beings (as in Beauvoir's *Pyrrhus et Cinéas*).

Thus Beauvoir argues that human beings constitute for each other the facticity of each other's situation. This means that they mutually form the necessary connection between human beings and the world which cannot be chosen and which is part of the always already situated-ness of human beings in time, space, etc.

Overall, Beauvoir's emphasis is on the reciprocal possibilities of self–Other relations in *Pyrrhus et Cinéas*. However, there is a brief discussion of violence, in which she does not condemn its use outright. She argues that sometimes violence may be necessary against those who seek to oppress, although it is always undesirable because it destroys equality, which is necessary for reciprocity to exist between transcendent human beings (Bergoffen 1997: 55–58). The issue of violence in

THE BLOOD OF OTHERS (1945)

Published a year after *Pyrrhus et Cinéas*, Beauvoir's second novel *The Blood of Others* (1945) is considered by some to be a fictional primer to her philosophical text. Set mainly in the 1930s and during the Second World War, the text opens on the ethical dilemma of a Resistance leader, Jean Blomart, as to whether to sanction further acts of sabotage which will necessarily result in German reprisals against the French population. In reaching his decision, Jean revisits key episodes in his past, analysing his past choices and the negative impact they have had on his relationships with others. Narrated by Jean and Hélène Bertrand, the text examines the nature of our relationship to others in a skilful analysis of how personal 'histoire' (story, history) becomes interwoven with collective history. In accordance with the text's Dostoyevskian epigraph ('each of us is responsible for everything and to every human being' from *The Brothers Karamazov* (1880)), Jean and Hélène, along with other characters in the novel, come to recognise the necessity of committed action and of assuming their responsibility towards the Other.

an erotic context will subsequently be addressed in both *The Second Sex* and in 'Must we burn Sade?' Elsewhere, in Beauvoir's fiction, the use of violence is explored in the context of Resistance actions in wartime France in *The Blood of Others* and in broader historical contexts in *All Men Are Mortal* and *The Mandarins*.

In *The Prime of Life*, the second volume of her memoirs published in France in 1960, Beauvoir explains that, in *Pyrrhus et Cinéas*, she had attempted to reconcile her differences with Sartre over the issue of 'situation'. She explains her distinction between natural freedom and moral freedom, the latter rooted in her recognition that 'actual concrete possibilities [of freedom] vary from one person to the next' (*PL*: 549). This crucial recognition of a hierarchy of different situations with different material consequences which impinge on an individual's possibilities of freedom is introduced in *Pyrrhus et Cinéas* and developed further in her subsequent works, *The Ethics of Ambiguity* and *The Second Sex*. In this way, Beauvoir develops an alternative to the absolutist notion of freedom explored in *Being and Nothingness*, where Sartre notes: 'Man can not be sometimes slave and sometimes free; he is wholly and forever free or he is not free at all' (*BN*: 441). Beauvoir's notion of freedom, however, is that it is 'situated' and dependent on an individual's relative capacity for action.

THE ETHICS OF AMBIGUITY

In 1947, with the publication of *The Ethics of Ambiguity*, Beauvoir further developed her distinct notion of the importance of the Other in 'situation'. In so doing, she signals an important engagement with the Heideggerian notion of '*Mitsein*' or 'being-with-others', which is largely absent from Sartre's *Being and Nothingness*.

In *The Ethics of Ambiguity*, Beauvoir begins her discussion by arguing that the human condition is ambiguous, by which she means that the meaning of human existence is not fixed, but must be constantly created within the parameters of seemingly opposed conditions of existence.

Gothlin has traced Beauvoir's use of the concept of ambiguity to her interpretation of Heidegger's notions of '*Erschlossenheit*' (disclosedness) and '*Mitsein*' (being-with-others) as well as to her rereading of Sartre's notion of the human being as a 'desire of being'(Gothlin in O'Brien and Embree 2001). Gothlin argues that, unlike Sartre, Beauvoir does not

AMBIGUITY

Ambiguity is a major concept in Beauvoir's thought and constitutes a fundamental characteristic of human existence that resists easy definition. It involves 'an irreducible indeterminacy and multiple, inseparable significations and aspects' (Langer in Card 2003: 90). Human existence is ambiguous because human beings are both free and unfree, separate and connected to each other, a subject for ourselves and an object for others, consciousness and body, alive yet born to die. Two important examples of ambiguity in Beauvoir's thought are that (1) human beings are both separate from and dependent on other people, and (2) women experience their embodiment and desire as ambiguous (to be examined in Chapter 3).

see the human condition as a 'useless passion', but rather, following Heidegger, as a desire to disclose being. She links freedom and disclosure: 'to will freedom and to will to disclose being are one and the same choice' (*EA*: 78). This means, as we shall see, that Beauvoir envisages freedom as only being realised by actively engaging itself in the world. In other words, we cannot just sit about and passively proclaim our freedom – we have to go out and actively use that freedom in the world and in our relationships with other people.

In part of the first section of *The Ethics of Ambiguity*, Beauvoir defends Sartrean existentialism, much in the same manner as her essay, 'L'Existentialisme et la sagesse des nations', first published in *Les Temps Modernes* at the end of 1945. Although such defences of existentialism have probably encouraged Sartrean readings of Beauvoir's philosophy, it is worth noting why they were deemed necessary. As noted in Chapter 1, by the mid 1940s, existentialism was not merely a philosophy, but a philosophy-lifestyle, which had infiltrated the '*Zeitgeist*', or 'spirit of the time', its wider influence evident in literature, the visual arts and music. From 1945 until around 1948, existentialism was attacked as a decadent, idealistic and bourgeois philosophy by the Catholic Church, the Communist Party and various right-wing groups, afraid of losing their influence over French society.

Engaging with these attacks in *The Ethics of Ambiguity*, Beauvoir addresses herself particularly to the accusation that existentialism is a subjective if not a solipsistic philosophy. She argues that existentialism's focus on the individual's assumption of his or her own freedom is a moral act, which necessarily implicates others' freedom. Here Beauvoir distinguishes, importantly, between the subject's natural freedom, which is the spontaneous, contingent freedom of coming into existence, and moral freedom, grounded by a project. This latter type of freedom implies the existence of the Other.

Beginning her discussion of freedom and situation with an analysis of the situation of children, Beauvoir argues that children live in a world which they have had no power to shape – it simply appears to be a given state of affairs, regulated by fixed adult values. In this way, the situation of the child is metaphysically privileged, for he or she is usually protected from experiencing existential anguish and is mostly able to avoid any serious consequences of his or her actions. Similarly, Beauvoir argues that there are certain groups of people in society who are obliged to live in an infantile world, because they have been kept in a state of slavery and ignorance, such as black slaves in the southern American states or women in patriarchal societies (*EA*: 37–38). She points out that, whereas the child's situation is imposed upon him or her, (Western) women choose, or at least consent to, their situation. Such a possibility of choice or consent needs to be differentiated from the possibilities of action found in the situation of a black slave in the eighteenth century or a Muslim woman forced to remain in a harem, both of whom, according to Beauvoir, have no real means of challenging their oppression. Their position has to be judged according to their relative possibilities of action. It makes no sense to say glibly that they are free, for they have no possibility of seizing that freedom. A key point to note here is Beauvoir's notion that there exist 'privileged situations' in which an individual can realise his or her freedom, and other situations in which freedom and one's capacity for action are severely limited, if they exist at all. But, once the possibility of freedom exists, the chance to act must be seized or the danger of 'bad faith' looms!

SOLIPSISM

Solipsism (from the Latin '*solus ipse*' – oneself alone) is a philosophical doctrine that advocates that only oneself exists. It includes two positions: (1) that one is the only self or centre of consciousness, and (2) that nothing at all exists apart from one's own mind and mental states or at least cannot be known or held to be true.

Beauvoir argues – unsurprisingly and in accordance with a broad existentialist premise that 'existence precedes essence' – that the child does not contain the future adult. But it is always on the basis of the past that an individual makes choices regarding future behaviour. Although the 'original choice' – or synthesising thread of a range of life choices – made by an individual can be reversed or remade, it is not without significance because the world reflects back to us our earlier choices. Consider the following example: despite all careers advice to the contrary, a person might decide that they want to be a lighthouse keeper even though there might only be two staffed lighthouses left in the country. They want to be a lighthouse keeper because in fact they find it very difficult to get on with other people. Competition for the vacancy of one of only two posts of lighthouse keeper in the country is quite stiff, but this person is utterly determined and manages to get the job. Working as a lighthouse keeper entails having to move four hundred miles away from friends and family, who are very puzzled by this decision because there are better job prospects in the same town. A few years later, the lighthouse keeper is made redundant, a casualty of computer technology. Returning to their home town and unable to find a job, the ex-lighthouse keeper finds that they have completely lost touch with family and friends, and they drift into a life of crime. The lighthouse keeper has consequently made several choices which have removed them from their social network, which, in turn, rejects them. The ex-lighthouse keeper then compounds their rejection by pursuing a life of crime, which alienates them further from society. The 'original choice' of turning their back on society might be remade, but it will become increasingly difficult as that 'original choice' is repeatedly 'acted out' in their life choices. So, in this way, it becomes increasingly difficult for us (whether we want to be lighthouse keepers or not!) to escape the consequences of such temporally situated choices because, as we grow older, we become more and more embroiled in the chess game of decisions which shape our lives.

In the second part of *The Ethics of Ambiguity*, Beauvoir offers a series of examples of 'bad faith' or ways in which particular types of people avoid their freedom, similar to Albert Camus's various portraits of the absurd man in *The Myth of Sisyphus*. But in *The Ethics of Ambiguity*, in a move which differentiates her position from that of Camus, Beauvoir clearly explains the difference between an absurd existence (which she rejects) and an ambiguous one (which she endorses): 'to declare existence absurd is to deny that it can ever be given a meaning; to say that it is ambiguous is to assert that its meaning is never fixed' (*EA*: 129). This is an explicit rejection, on Beauvoir's part, of nihilism or that nothing has any value. Instead, each individual has to assume the responsibility of their freedom and create meaning through their choices and, hence, attempt to avoid bad faith.

Towards the end of Part II, Beauvoir again rejects a conflictual model of self–Other relations, derived originally from the Hegelian master–slave dialectic (see Chapter 1, pp. 16–17) and interpreted rather pessimistically by Sartre in *Being and Nothingness*. She cites the epigraph which she used for her first novel, *She Came to Stay*, from Hegel's *Phenomenology of Spirit* – 'each consciousness pursues the death of the other' – and argues that this hatred can only be a naive, preliminary reaction to the Other, because the Other simultaneously takes and *gives* the world to me.

While we might need others, however, our relationships with them are complex and, in the third main section of *The Ethics of Ambiguity*, Beauvoir examines various factors relating to oppressive relationships.

She observes that it is the 'interdependence' within our relationships with others which explains how oppression is possible (*EA*: 82). She focuses upon the effect of oppression on the material reality of people's lives and its power to crush their physical, psychological and emotional capacity for resistance and authentic action.

In *Being and Nothingness*, however, while Sartre at no point denies the existence of obstacles to freedom, he argues that we choose how to interpret such obstacles. Sartre's overestimation of individual will and choice even when faced with crushing oppression leads him to the inhumane and abstract position from which he argues that those who submit under torture do so freely, and that a Jew is free to choose whether to accept his or her oppression at the hands of anti-Semitic people (*BN*: 524).

In *The Ethics of Ambiguity*, Beauvoir analyses how we can struggle for the freedom of others – by helping them to reach a position where they can assume their freedom – yet she recognises that assisting some people in certain circumstances is often to act simultaneously against others. There are privileged courses of action in the struggle for freedom: for example, Beauvoir acknowledges that it is more appropriate that black people struggle for other black people, Jews for Jews, women for other women, and so on. To belong to an oppressed group is to have *lived experience* of oppression that cannot be shared by an individual who chooses to express solidarity with the struggle of another oppressed individual. This phenomenological understanding of oppression, with its focus on the lived experience of oppression, will be crucial in *The Second Sex* and in *Old Age*.

In this way, by making reference to contemporary political situations of the 1940s, such as the German Occupation of France and the oppression of the black population in the US, Beauvoir provides historical examples relevant to some of the key notions associated with existentialism, such as the politics of freedom and the complexities of the self–Other relation. Anticipating her later work in *The Second Sex*, she also makes connections between different types of oppression, such as anti-Semitism, sexism and racism.

In *The Ethics of Ambiguity*, Beauvoir seeks to provide an existentialist ethics, which 'is experienced in the truth of life' (*EA*: 159). The practical value and relevance of existentialism was important to Beauvoir. Describing her reading of Hegel in 1940, in the midst of Occupied

Paris, she observes that, once she had stepped out of the library, his philosophical system was of no use to her: 'what it had showed me, under a show of the infinite, was the consolations of death' (*EA*: 158).

ETHICS AND THE EROTIC

Beauvoir returned to examine ethical questions in relation to the erotic in two essays published in the 1950s, 'Must we burn Sade?' (1951–1952) and 'Brigitte Bardot and the Lolita syndrome' (1959). It may seem odd to some readers that Beauvoir, as a feminist and a keen analyst of women's situation and oppression in patriarchal society, would be interested in the writings of the Marquis de Sade, known for his sexual sadism and transgressive erotic writings. Beauvoir was, however, in good company, as Sade was a key reference point in the twentieth century for literary theorists such as Roland Barthes (1915–1980), Georges Bataille (1897–1962) and Maurice Blanchot (1907–2003).

So why was Beauvoir interested in Sade? It is important to note that she does not condone Sade or see him as any kind of ethical model, but she does recognise that his life and work tell us something significant about the limits and possibilities of human sexuality, power and embodiment. Although Beauvoir and Sade were working within very different political and ethical contexts, they both defended sexual freedom and viewed sexuality not as a biological imperative, but as a social fact. Beauvoir saw that Sade had turned his own subversive, sadistic sexuality into an ethic or mode of living and expressed that ethic of the erotic in his writing. In this way, although Sade's case is

MARQUIS DE SADE (1740–1814)

The Marquis de Sade was a French writer, libertine and atheist, imprisoned for much of his life for his political, but mainly sexual, subversion. Although Sade wrote in a variety of genres, such as prose narrative, drama, political tracts and philosophical treatises, he is perhaps best known for his shocking novels, in which he explores crimes, perversions, erotic pleasure and power in uncensored detail. For many generations a forbidden author, Sade is now considered important as a writer and theorist of transgression.

extreme and morally reprehensible, it is also one which, in Beauvoir's view, is instructive in its charting of the possibilities of erotic transgression and what such transgression implies for our relationships with the Other.

In her essay, 'Must we burn Sade?', Beauvoir examines Sade's life briefly, interprets his eroticism in his literary texts and examines his (im)moral doctrine. She views him as a member of the nobility who sought to synthesise the violent and arbitrary justice of the aristocracy with bourgeois rationalism through his pursuit of an ethic of the erotic. But, crucially, she regards Sade as a 'noble failure' in that he fails to experience reciprocal intersubjectivity: his universe is solipsistic and the reality of the Other is denied. Sade, however, 'posed the problem of the other in its extremest terms; in his excesses, man-as-transcendence and man-as-object achieve a dramatic confrontation' (*PL*: 255). Few writers had shown the possibilities of egoism, tyranny and cruelty in sexual love. In the theatre of the erotic, Sade shows how the interests of master and slave can be irreconcilable and, in this, according to Beauvoir, he anticipates the class struggle. She sees Sade's extreme sexual preferences as attempting to compensate for being unable to experience emotional intoxication in sexual love (*MBS*: 33). Sade is simply unable to 'lose himself' in the erotic encounter with the Other. His satisfactions can only be obtained in an imaginary (literary) world, in which others as embodied consciousnesses did not exist for him. For Beauvoir argues in 'Must we burn Sade?' that:

> the state of emotional intoxication allows one to grasp existence in one's self and in the other, as both subjectivity and passivity. The two partners merge in this ambiguous unity; each one is freed of his own presence and achieves immediate communication with the other.
>
> (*MBS*: 33)

The erotic relation is a privileged situation in that we encounter the Other both as body and as consciousness. But, in Sade's solipsistic imaginary universe, emotion is absent and eroticism loses its value as a unique shared experience. All that is left are abstract figures and vulgar biological representations. Nevertheless, even if he failed, Beauvoir argues that Sade was trying to elaborate an ethic of authenticity in his theorisation of the erotic. Sade's value is to have explored the transgressive possibilities of the erotic encounter and by so doing,

BRIGITTE BARDOT (1934–)

Brigitte Bardot, a French film actress known as 'BB' ('Bébé' or 'baby'), is particularly associated with sexy, if misogynist, roles in films of the 1950s and 1960s, exemplified by Roger Vadim's *And God Created Woman* (*Et Dieu créa la femme*) (1957), and by Jean-Luc Godard's *Contempt* (*Le Mépris*) (1963). Bardot retired from cinema in 1973 to devote herself – somewhat ironically – to animal welfare.

argues Beauvoir, he forces us to confront the parameters of the self–Other relation.

So, both Beauvoir and Sade link the question of ethics with the erotic body (Bergoffen 1997: 39). In Sade's case, erotic desire enacted as solipsism and tyranny precludes reciprocal self–Other relations and the possibility of authentic action and rebellion (Butler in Card 2003: 170). For Beauvoir, however, erotic desire and exchange potentially involve a reciprocal encounter between embodied consciousnesses who are ethically implicated with each other – the erotic relation acts as an ethical building block which is part of a broader social and ethical relation.

Beauvoir then took up some of these issues in her short essay, 'Brigitte Bardot and the Lolita syndrome' (1959). Drawing on her work on myth from *The Second Sex* (see Chapter 3, p. 64), Beauvoir argues that Brigitte Bardot constitutes (literally) a new embodiment of the old myth of 'the eternal feminine' in Vadim's *And God Created Woman* (*BB*: 8). This has been less successful in France than in America because American men, according to Beauvoir, are less threatened by the sexual equality implied by Bardot's sexually liberated behaviour (*BB*: 22–23). Although she was a huge hit in the US and hence, according to Beauvoir, as important a French 'export' as Renault cars, Bardot was subjected to a volley of accusations of immorality levelled at her in the French press.

In her essay, Beauvoir is interested in the disruptive erotic power of Bardot as a combination of 'femme fatale' and 'nymphette'. Although Vadim, director of *And God Created Woman*, positions the spectator as 'voyeur', Beauvoir reads Bardot both on and off screen as resistant to being positioned as the fetishised body-object of the male gaze, leaving its bearer feeling cheated and vindictive (*BB*: 30). The male

AND GOD CREATED WOMAN (1957)

Renamed by some feminists as 'And Man Created Tart', And God Created Woman is set in St Tropez and depicts Juliette, a highly-sexualised, 18-year-old nymphette who is deemed incomprehensible by all except an older man who, obsessed by her, seeks to keep her in his sight and protect her to the point of arranging her marriage to a man she does not love. The viewer is encouraged to identify with the gaze of the older man that consumes and polices the body of Bardot, which is 'always there to be speculated' (Hayward 1993: 177). Bardot dances her way around St Tropez, culminating in a final sequence of Latin American dancing which, shot in close-up from the waist down, is blatant in its objectification of the female body for consumption by an implied heterosexual male voyeur.

gaze is also frustrated by Vadim's analytical style, which fails to render the story or characters at all convincing and which heightens the effect of Bardot's 'aggressive' femininity. As in 'Must we burn Sade?', the erotic encounter in *And God Created Woman* is represented as devoid of humanity and reciprocity (Vintges 1996: 49). It is, then, a failed ethical encounter. Although Bardot's possibilities of genuine sexual autonomy in post-war French cinema are rightly contested by more recent feminist film critics, Beauvoir was correct to identify her subversive erotic power, even if it is a power contained and manipulated by the patriarchal gaze both on and off screen (Hayward 1993: 177–178). Like Sade (though in reverse!) Bardot challenges the consuming tyranny of the patriarchal gaze and ultimately loses, but again, it is, in Beauvoir's eyes, a 'noble failure' which helps us reflect on the ethics of the erotic bond between self and Other.

In *Pyrrhus et Cinéas*, *The Ethics of Ambiguity* and her essays on Sade and Bardot, Beauvoir introduces and develops key concepts such as the Other, ambiguity, situation, disclosure and appeal. These are further developed within the context of gender relations in *The Second Sex*. This ground-breaking study of women's condition will be the focus of the next chapter.

SUMMARY

In *Pyrrhus et Cinéas* and *The Ethics of Ambiguity*, Beauvoir introduces and develops several key concepts, such as situation, reciprocity, ambiguity, disclosure and appeal which inform her analyses of women's condition in *The Second Sex*. She distances herself from Sartre's conflictual account of self–Other relations, emphasising the reciprocal possibilities of our self–Other interdependence, the importance of situation and the moral aspects of freedom. In 'Must we burn Sade?' and 'Brigitte Bardot and the Lolita syndrome', she argues that the erotic encounter with the Other is a privileged ethical situation in which reciprocal recognition can and should exist.

3

BECOMING WOMAN

This chapter introduces the key ideas of *The Second Sex*, the work for which Simone de Beauvoir is most well known. *The Second Sex* was published in France in 1949, five years after French women finally gained the right to vote.

WOMEN'S SUFFRAGE

Women gained the right to vote in France in 1944. This compares unfavourably to Britain: 1918 for women over 30, 1928 for women over 21; US: 1920; New Zealand: 1893; Australia: 1908; Norway: 1913; Finland: 1906; Soviet Union: 1917; Germany, Austria, Poland, the Netherlands: 1919; and Spain: 1931.

The delay in according women the right to vote in France can be explained by several factors: first, until the mid twentieth century, a pro-natalist policy was widely supported by all major political parties, including the Communists and Socialists, in a bid to increase the birth rate and tackle a major depopulation crisis. Contraception and abortion were consequently both illegal, and there was huge political and social pressure on women to conform to the traditional roles of wife and mother. Astonishingly, French women were still considered legal minors until 1938, and it would take until the 1960s and 1970s for women to gain the right to contraception (1967), abortion (1974) and to engage in paid work and open a bank account without the authorisation of their husband (1965). Second, women as a voting block were perceived by many left-wing politicians (who were the most likely to support the campaign for female suffrage) to be more religious, so there was a widespread fear that, if women were given the right to vote, they would simply follow the conservative directives of the Catholic Church which opposed left-wing policies. Finally, the women's suffrage movement was itself not a militant campaign in France (precisely because of the strong influence of the Catholic Church over women) and was therefore less effective in achieving its aims (Duchen 1986: 3). This contrasted with the British suffrage campaign which, for many years, involved extensive direct political action, such as hunger strikes, acts of sabotage and violent self-sacrifice, such as that of Emily Wilding Davison, who hurled herself under the King's horse in a Derby Day race in 1913 (Anderson and Zinsser 1990: 363–366).

In France, then, a range of factors had combined to delay the granting of votes for women and to maintain them in a state of subordination to men. Additionally, during the German Occupation of France during the Second World War (1939–1945), the provisional French government, based at Vichy, which adopted a policy of collaboration with the Nazi regime, introduced stringent measures that further circumscribed women's autonomy, such as dismissing all married working women from their jobs, denouncing all non-childbearing women and strengthening the sanctions in existing legislation which outlawed abortion and contraception.

So it was in this context that Beauvoir began work on *The Second Sex* in 1946 – at a time when the majority of French women were still being pressurised into becoming wives and mothers, had little control over their own fertility and expression of their sexuality, were unable to assume their financial autonomy and were discriminated against in the labour market.

Described as 'one of the most criticised *and* one of the least read works in feminism' (Vintges 1996: 21–22) and as 'a major philosophical text and the deepest and most original work of feminist thought to have been produced in this century' (Moi 1999: vii), for over fifty years *The Second Sex* has been the focus of debate and dispute. Its wide-ranging and sophisticated analyses of women's situation draw on existential phenomenology and anthropology, combined with a Marxist analysis of history, as well as providing an early feminist critique of classical psychoanalysis. If we were to summarise her text in two concepts, these would be:

* woman is the absolute Other; and
* femininity is constructed.

But how she develops these concepts needs more explanation!

THE SECOND SEX: A GENERAL OVERVIEW

The Second Sex is divided into two volumes: the first is entitled *Facts and Myths*; the second, *Woman's Life Today*, although a philosophically correct translation of the latter would be *Lived Experience*, reflecting Beauvoir's phenomenological approach (McBride in Simons 1999: 70). Overall, it focuses on how femininity has been conceptualised and how women 'become' relative beings in a patriarchal society. Its main argument is that, throughout history, 'woman' has been constructed as man's Other and denied access to an autonomous existence. Men have positioned themselves as uniquely responsible for all aspects of public life and correspondingly women have been confined to a margin-alised position in society according to which they are made to support male interests. Beauvoir argues that man has assumed the position of universal subject, and woman is positioned as relative 'Other', or object of male consciousness. Society is consequently structured to perpetuate patriarchal ideology and women are maintained in an inferior position. This persistence of patriarchal ideology throughout history has enabled men to assume that they have a right to maintain women in a subordinate state and women have internalised and adapted to this oppressed state. Beauvoir argues that both men and women perpetuate patriarchy, which is why it is able to continue.

Sexual oppression continues because, according to Beauvoir, gender roles are learned from the very earliest age and reinforced perpetually. The famous phrase that opens the second volume of *The Second Sex*, 'One is not born, but rather becomes, a woman', means that there is no pre-established female nature or essence. Here, Beauvoir adapts existentialism's notion of 'existence precedes essence' to the ways in which gender identity is experienced. There only appear to be distinct

and determining male or female identities because society has traditionally organised itself according to a sexual apartheid or segregation,
rooted in men's and women's different biological make-up and reproductive roles. For example, the fact that, to a lesser or greater degree
in the world, patriarchal societies traditionally value women's reproductive capacity more than her intellectual development or autonomy,
means that laws, institutions and belief systems reflect this view of
women's role in society.

Beauvoir accepts that there are certain minor physiological and
biological differences between women and men. A common misreading
of *The Second Sex* is that she does not recognise sexual difference and
thinks that women should become like men in their quest for freedom.
In fact, Beauvoir recognises sexual difference, but does not accept that
the valuing of these differences between women and men should justify
the oppression of women and their traditional status as second-class
citizens in patriarchal society.

For Beauvoir, society is organised in such a way as to favour male
projects and aspirations. The obvious question which arises is: How did
such a system come into being? In *The Second Sex*, Beauvoir provides a
thorough survey of the origins and perpetuation of the patriarchal
oppression of women. She explains that, since the beginning of social
organisation, men, as physically stronger beings, were better adapted
to heavy manual work involved in hunting, fishing and defending the
tribe. Women were involved in domestic work and raising children.
Men consequently had more freedom to invent systems of thought and
social and political organisation because they did not bear children.
These conceptual, social and political systems then developed to favour
male interests rather than society's interests as a whole. Women have
been obliged to adapt to this patriarchal system, which maintains them
in a subordinate position.

Beauvoir argues that women have been assimilated to their body and
sexed identity and traditionally confined to the roles of wife and
mother. Marriage and motherhood have consequently been artificially
promoted as the most important roles for women in society and this
has been inscribed in the laws, customs, beliefs and culture of society.
As a result, women have been traditionally prevented from working
outside the home and, hence, have been obliged to attach themselves
to a male breadwinner to ensure their survival and that of their children. Women have adapted to this state of affairs in a variety of ways

which encourage 'inauthenticity' to a lesser or greater extent. Beauvoir argues that the way forward for women is to pursue economic independence through independent work and through a socialist organisation of society, which would favour women's emancipation and autonomy.

FACTS AND MYTHS

Let's now look at *The Second Sex* in more detail. In the introduction to the first volume, Beauvoir starts out by stating that woman is a transcendent being who, like man, should live as an authentic subject and allow others to do the same (Lundgren-Gothlin 1996: 184). As noted in Chapter 2, freedom is both an individual and collective undertaking: 'to will oneself free is also to will others free' (*EA*: 73). Freedom implies transcendence and responsibility: 'to be free is not to have the power to do anything you like; it is to be able to surpass the given toward an open future' (*EA*: 91). So the fact that 'woman [. . .] finds herself living in a world where men compel her to assume the status of the Other' and is deprived of her transcendence in patriarchal societies is, in Beauvoir's view, quite simply unethical (*SS*: 29). Building on her work in *Pyrrhus et Cinéas* and *The Ethics of Ambiguity*, she defines her approach to analysing women's situation as that of existentialist ethics. Consequently, Beauvoir will be less interested in questions of gender identity in *The Second Sex* – we have seen that she rejects any notion that a fixed gender identity exists – and much more concerned with questions of power and behaviour in gender relations. In other words, how do the ways in which we behave towards each other confirm or challenge power inequalities between the genders? For example, you might want to think about the following questions: Are heterosexual women judged differently to heterosexual men if they have multiple sexual partners? Are men encouraged to view domestic work and parenting as essential to their roles as partners, husbands and employees? Are women paid less than men for work of the same value and importance in the labour market? Has this always been the case? If so, why? If not, why not? All these issues are informed by how gender politics affect our personal and professional relationships, and it is precisely the structuring and elaboration of the power dynamic in gender relations which preoccupies Beauvoir in *The Second Sex*.

In addition to an existentialist ethical framework, Beauvoir also adopts a Marxist analysis of history in her analysis of the situation of women. Seeking an explanation for the origins of woman's oppression, she argues that historical 'evidence' is not reliable or conclusive because it is produced by men to justify their oppression of women. Instead she proposes that, following Hegel's account of the master–slave dialectic, we might interpret woman's position as absolute 'Other' as the result of a process of 'becoming'. She argues that 'to be' a woman should be interpreted in the dynamic Hegelian sense of 'to have become' (SS: 24). Although conflict between men and women may have been at the source of this positioning of woman, Beauvoir says there has also always been a Heideggerian 'Mitsein', or 'being-with-others', in the relationship between women and men, which explains how women have never been consistently positioned as Other in the same way as other marginalised groups. For, unlike Jews or black people living in the southern states of the US in the 1940s, women have never constituted a minority group with a distinctive identity:

> They [women] have no past, no history, no religion of their own [. . .] they live dispersed among the males, attached through residence, housework, economic condition, and social standing to certain men – fathers or husbands – more firmly than they are to other women. If they belong to the bourgeoisie, they feel solidarity with men of that class, not with proletarian women; if they are white, their allegiance is to white men, not negro women [. . .] the bond that unites her [woman] to her oppressors is not comparable to any other. The division of the sexes is a biological fact, not an event in human history.
>
> (SS: 19)

However, in The Second Sex, the biological 'facts' of woman's situation are themselves not immune from masculinist bias on occasions, as we will see below.

It is worth noting here that Beauvoir argues that 'no group ever sets itself up as the One without at once setting up the Other over against itself' – in other words, every time a group comes into existence, it positively differentiates itself from those not within its number. For example, the power dynamics of any school playground illustrate this separation of 'selves' from 'others', as children form groups based on perceived differences within the larger social group. Noting Hegel's account of the master–slave dialectic, Beauvoir says that 'we find in consciousness itself a fundamental hostility towards every other consciousness, the subject can be posed only in being opposed – he sets himself up as the essential, as opposed to the other, the inessential, the object' (*SS*: 17). So the division of people into selves and others is fairly inevitable, but the specific relationship between men and women is of a special kind.

In her study of the philosophical sources of *The Second Sex*, Eva Lundgren-Gothlin argues that Beauvoir does not position man as master and woman as slave in her use of the Hegelian master–slave dialectic (Lundgren-Gothlin 1996: 68–76). Reading Hegel through Kojève, she argues that women do not participate in the Hegelian struggle for recognition, which takes place only between men. Lundgren-Gothlin notes that Beauvoir works with two different notions of 'otherness': the master–slave conflict which seeks to establish self and Other among men, and the non-dialectical relationship of self and absolute Other between men and women – a relationship rooted in their biological and psychological dependence on each other. So, while woman is 'Other' to man as universal subject, she is not the same type of 'Other' as other men against whom man seeks to define himself. As we saw above, woman is the absolute Other because of the special nature of her relationship to her oppressor through a combination of economic, emotional, domestic and social bonds. In formulating her notion of woman as absolute Other, Beauvoir also drew on work by the contemporary anthropologist, Claude Lévi-Strauss, who argued in *Les Structures élémentaires de la parenté* (*The Elementary Structures of Kinship*) (1949) that men always use women as 'instruments of exchange' among themselves to retain their social power. Women, consequently, always remain defined as absolute Other to men who position themselves as universal subjects.

CLAUDE LEVI-STRAUSS (1908–)

A contemporary of Sartre and Beauvoir and similarly trained in philosophy, Lévi-Strauss combined social anthropology with structuralism (see Chapter 5, p. 91) in several influential works, such as *Les Structures élémentaires de la parenté* (1949), *Tristes tropiques* (1955), *La Pensée sauvage* (1962) and *Mythologiques* (1964–1971). Beauvoir signalled her interest in Lévi-Strauss's account of kinship and myth in a laudatory review in *Les Temps Modernes* in November 1949.

DISCOURSE

'Discourse' is used here in the sense attributed to it by the French philosopher, Michel Foucault (1926–1984) to mean 'historically variable ways of specifying knowledge and truth – what it is possible to speak of at a given moment' (Ramazanoglu 1993: 19). Discourses, in this sense, work as sets of rules which govern the distribution of power and the production of truth. In his work, such as *Madness and Civilisation* (1961) and *The History of Sexuality* (published from 1976), Foucault was interested in how discursive formations such as 'madness' and 'sexuality' come into being and how subjects are discursively constituted.

In the first volume of *The Second Sex*, divided into three parts entitled 'Destiny', History' and 'Myths', Beauvoir examines how femininity is understood and represented. She focuses initially on three dominant 'forces', or 'discourses' (as we might describe them today), namely biology, psychoanalysis and Marxism, to understand what it is to be a woman. These were the three main explanatory physiological, psychological and economic theories of subjectivity and social relations in the 1940s.

Beauvoir begins by focusing on biology because it was and remains a linchpin in theories of sexual difference. Opponents of feminism usually base their arguments on biological difference to justify sexual oppression. Reading *The Second Sex* today, it is important also to remember that it was written before French women had access to legalised contraception and abortion, as noted earlier, and so heterosexual women had less control over their fertility than today.

BIOLOGY AND EMBODIED EXPERIENCE

Beauvoir's main argument concerning women's biology is that women have been obliged to experience their body as facticity rather than contingency: this means that women do not choose how they 'exist' their bodies (see next paragraph) because their embodiment has been pre-defined by patriarchal society. Woman's relationship to her body is therefore culturally produced. Beauvoir's view of embodied existence in *The Second Sex* draws on Sartre's account of the body in *Being and Nothingness* and Maurice Merleau-Ponty's description of the

MAURICE MERLEAU-PONTY (1908–1961)

Merleau-Ponty was a philosopher and essayist who, like Sartre and Beauvoir, transformed early French post-war philosophy by drawing on the work of Husserl and Heidegger. He was a close contemporary of Beauvoir and Sartre and was political editor of *Les Temps Modernes*. His best-known work is *Phenomenology of Perception* (1945), in which he took the situated embodied subject as his point of departure to explore our lived embodied experience and the ambiguity of our interrelationships with ourselves, others and the world. Merleau-Ponty was critical of Sartre's emphasis on consciousness and absolutist notion of freedom in *Being and Nothingness*. Like Sartre and Beauvoir, he sought to reconcile existentialism and Marxism, but became increasingly disillusioned with the orthodoxy of the French Communist Party.

embodied subject in *Phenomenology of Perception*, although many Beauvoir scholars agree that it is closer to the latter (see Bergoffen 1997; Heinämaa in Card 2003; Kruks 1990, 1992; Moi 1994; Tidd 1999; Vintges 1996).

In a review of Merleau-Ponty's *Phenomenology of Perception* in *Les Temps Modernes* (1945), Beauvoir welcomed his view of subjectivity as always already incarnate. His concept of the body was close to her notion of the female body as expressive of 'situation' and distinct from Sartre's account in *Being and Nothingness* of embodied consciousness as effectively striving towards its own perpetual self-disembodiment. For Sartre argues that the body is the physical evidence of what consciousness hasse been or transcended (*BN*: 309, 326). Consciousness *exists* the body, which means that, according to Sartre, the body is not an object of consciousness. This notion of the body raises a number of problems, which are addressed by Beauvoir in *The Second Sex* and by Merleau-Ponty in *Phenomenology of Perception*.

The first problem is that Sartre's view of the body is rather abstract. It neglects the lived experience of how we experience, and are sometimes encouraged to experience, our bodies. For example, his concept of the body in *Being and Nothingness* cannot account for the experience and power politics of living as a black transgendered person in a white supremacist patriarchy, which entail potentially oppressive implications on material, psychological and social levels. Beauvoir was precisely interested in how power relations govern this 'lived experience' of embodied subjectivity and how our body might be expressions of that experience in the world.

The second related problem is that Sartre's account tends to view the body as a passive instrument subject to the mind's wilful control. This neglects some of the sophisticated ways in which we can experience our bodies, psychologically and physiologically, and the relation of these experiences to socio-political bodily interdictions. For example, in *Phenomenology of Perception*, Merleau-Ponty explores cases of amputees and brain-damaged people who experience their bodies differently (Merleau-Ponty 1962: 76–87, 103). He argues that there are two layers to bodily reality: the habitual body and the present body (Merleau-Ponty 1962: 82). The habitual body is the mode of existing our bodies based on past experience – gestures learned within a spatial and temporal context and, importantly, within an intersubjective context. The present body is the way in which we experience our bodies according to the demands of present and future contexts, which may require a relearning of our embodied subjectivity. In Merleau-Ponty's view, the body is an expression of our relationship with the world; it is always already anchored in space, time and in relation to others, and constitutes the point at which we assume our subjectivity in the world. Beauvoir largely agrees with Merleau-Ponty's view of the embodied subject and develops her own notion of the lived body and the represented body in the context of gender in *The Second Sex*. But Beauvoir helped to promote the view that her philosophy was closer to Sartre's than Merleau-Ponty's – for reasons of intellectual and emotional loyalty – and so, until recently, these connections between the philosophies of Beauvoir and Merleau-Ponty have been overlooked.

In her account of female biology in *The Second Sex*, Beauvoir adapts Merleau-Ponty's argument within the context of gender: 'Woman, like man, *is* her body; but her body is something other than herself' (*SS*: 61). This means that woman's experience of embodiment is separated from her transcendence and, in patriarchal society, which has traditionally promoted woman's objectification, she is rewarded for alienating (or reducing) her transcendent subjectivity to her physicality. In short, patriarchy furthers its aims by encouraging women to experience themselves as docile bodies for male consumption. While Beauvoir makes it clear in *The Second Sex* that woman's alienation in her body is not inevitable, her lurid portrayal of female biology nevertheless might appear rather deterministic. As Moi notes, 'for Beauvoir, women are the slaves of the species. Every biological process in the female body is a "crisis" or a "trial", and the result is always alienation' (Moi 1994: 165).

What is the explanation for this biological pessimism? In *The Second Sex*, Beauvoir sees 'biological data' as being crucial to an understanding of woman's situation, but she shows that the representation of such data is often informed by gender myths and stereotyping. Some commentators, however, such as Haddock Seigfried, argue that Beauvoir is a prisoner of the scientific discourses of her time, and slides into essentialism (the notion that there might be some inherent female essence) in her 'description' of female biology (Haddock Seigfried in Al-Hibri and Simons 1990: 319). More recently, Elizabeth Fallaize has argued that Beauvoir does not unconsciously reproduce the masculinist bias of the scientific discourses of the 1940s in the chapter on biology; she is concerned rather to dismantle certain biological myths and metaphors about the female in the natural world, which have prevented serious discussion of women's role in society (Fallaize in O'Brien and Embree 2001: 67–84).

PSYCHOANALYSIS

Beauvoir addresses the issue of sexuality in the following chapter on psychoanalysis and in the 'Formative years' section of the second volume. Here we will initially concentrate on why psychoanalysis is of interest to feminism generally and on Beauvoir's critique of psychoanalysis in the first volume of *The Second Sex*. As we shall see later in the next chapter, her reading of Freud and psychoanalytic accounts of subjectivity anticipates French and Anglo-Saxon feminist critiques of psychoanalysis, which developed from the 1970s.

You may be wondering why Beauvoir and feminism more generally would be interested in psychoanalysis? First, because of the importance of sexuality and gender in psychoanalytic theory. Psychoanalysis sees gender as central to the constitution of subjectivity; all identity is gendered for psychoanalysis. Feminism, similarly, is concerned with understanding gendered identity. Second, psychoanalysis is concerned with 'telling stories' in its use of 'the talking cure' and with the interpretation of those stories. Similarly, feminism is also concerned with analysing women's lives and the patriarchal system which shapes those

SIGMUND FREUD 1856–1939

Freud's work has shaped a whole climate of thought and opinion across many disciplines in the twentieth century. Viewed as a founder of psychoanalysis, a branch of psychology, established at the end of the nineteenth century, many of his original concepts, such as 'the unconscious', 'dream symbolism', 'projection' and 'repression', have passed into popular culture and opinions. Freud qualified as a doctor, but he was primarily interested in research into nervous diseases. In 1885, he went to Paris to study with Jean-Martin Charcot (1825–1893), a neurologist, who was working mainly with female hysterics and using hypnosis to classify and explain their behaviour. Freud thought that hysteria might be mentally produced and related to disturbances in infantile female sexuality. The psychoanalytic 'talking cure' involved (usually) women lying on a couch, often under hypnosis and 'free-associating', or saying whatever came into their heads. Many patients related episodes of childhood sexual abuse by figures in positions of paternal authority. Freud doubted that abuse could be so widespread and interpreted these experiences as possibly unconscious primal fantasy or the distorted fulfilment of a wish revealing itself in the stories he heard. He went on to develop influential theories of sexuality and sexual development and psychic life more generally, drawing on various case histories.

lives. For example, in the 1960s and 1970s, 'consciousness-raising' was an important part of feminism. This was a process through which women met in groups to articulate their own experiences as women in patriarchal society and to make connections between these personal experiences as a means to achieve political change. Feminism, at a very general level, then, is concerned with a similar set of problems to psychoanalysis.

So, what does Freud say about sexual development and why is it important for feminism? He argued that sexuality begins in infancy, especially through the child's relationship with his or her parents. According to Freud, our libido (basic instinctual sex drive) leads us towards a concentration of energetic excitement and a desire for release. The libido has three stages of focus: the oral, anal and phallic, or genital, stages. The baby begins life as 'polymorphously perverse', which means that he or she eroticises everything and wants everything and everyone who interests him or her. In infancy, the child makes no distinction between the outside world and the boundaries of its own body; it all merges into one 'pleasure zone' where desires are satisfied. But the infant soon realises that all her or his desires cannot be met. This plays out differently, according to psychoanalysis, depending on whether you are a boy or a girl. Freud claims that the child develops an attraction for the parent of the opposite sex and a jealous hatred for the other parent. The child becomes a girl or boy in terms of either the castration complex (for boys) or penis envy (for girls). This is part of the last genital, or phallic, phase of sexual development. The boy, having identified his penis as a source of pleasure, fears that his father, who is the rival to his affections for his mother, might take it away. The logic behind this fear is that the boy has realised that not all children have a penis – i.e., girls exist – and he assumes this may happen to him. But this fear resolves the Oedipus Complex (the process via which he had fallen in love with his mother) and the boy relinquishes his attraction for his mother. The girl, however, sees herself as already castrated – she sees herself as lacking a penis and wants one. She also realises that her mother, her primary love object, has no penis and therefore cannot supply her with one. The girl then turns to the father, who might be able to give her a penis or a baby. This means that the girl's incestuous desire is never resolved and women have a less well-developed super-ego (the child's internalisation of parental and cultural authority) because they have not internalised paternal authority to the same extent as men.

In the 'psychoanalysis' chapter of *The Second Sex* Beauvoir outlines these various phases of psychosexual development according to Freud. Her main criticisms are the following: first, that his account of female sexuality is grafted on to a male model, so that the girl can only consider herself as a mutilated boy (*SS*: 73–78). Beauvoir does not accept this universalist view of female sexuality or that girls value the penis in the way that Freud describes. Beauvoir argues that the girl's entire situation in patriarchal society contributes to her sense of inferiority, not simply the fact that she does not have a penis. She envies instead the privileges brought by the possession of a penis. Second, Beauvoir criticises Freud because he does not account for the social construction of the father as a dominant figure in patriarchal society.

Beauvoir argues that all psychoanalysts allot the same destiny to woman – that of undergoing a conflict between her masculine and feminine tendencies – so that, in asserting her independence within this binary, she can only become virilised. As an existentialist, Beauvoir views psychoanalysis as suppressing the notions of choice and value, and as a deterministic system which internalises human reality rather than viewing existence as a material experience which is lived in the world with other people. As already noted, situation and reciprocal relations with others are key factors in Beauvoir's notion of subjectivity. The emphasis on the past in psychoanalysis also conflicts with an existentialist notion of the ways in which we experience time, according to which the subject is simultaneously situated in *three* temporal dimensions (past, present and future). For Beauvoir, although we are radically separated from our past, as transcendent beings we must assume our existence as experienced in past, present and future to develop an authentic project in the world. So we cannot 'live in the past' or only anticipate tomorrow if we wish to live authentically because the past, present and future are constantly interwoven into our existence.

Beauvoir did, however, recognise Freud's 'discovery' of children's sexuality as highly significant, and she uses some psychoanalytic theory in her description of sexual development in the second volume of *The Second Sex*.

MARXISM

Beauvoir is more indulgent towards Marxism and uses several Marxist concepts in *The Second Sex*, such as 'alienation', and draws upon a Marxist analysis of history, as noted on p. 54. Chapter 3 of *The Second Sex* is devoted to 'historical materialism' and this concept is closely linked to Beauvoir's notion of 'becoming a woman'. A fundamental aspect which Beauvoir shares with Marxist thinking is the rejection of a given human nature: human nature is an historical and social product. Although there are few overt references to Marx in *The Second Sex*, Marxist ideas nevertheless permeate its analyses of gender identity and history.

In this chapter on historical materialism, Beauvoir initially argues that economic and social contexts are crucial in determining the importance attributed to the 'biological facts' of gender: in prehistoric times when physical strength was valued, women were rendered inferior, but the contemporary reliance on technology enables them to work on equal terms alongside men. Beauvoir concentrates mainly on the theories of Friedrich Engels (1820–1895), Marx's lifelong collaborator and editor, as the main representative of historical materialism. This is because it was Engels rather than Marx who concentrated on

'HISTORICAL MATERIALISM'

The term 'historical materialism' was first coined by Karl Marx (1818–1883) (see Chapter 1) to describe his method of social analysis which concentrated on class inequality. Historical materialism refers to the notion that human consciousness is determined by social and economic conditions. It focuses on the actual world in which real people live and argues that social inequalities are historically located and, hence, open to change. Historical materialism necessarily stands at odds with biologistic and psychological explanations of human oppression, seeing these as themselves products of social relations. Feminism holds by definition a materialist conception of human nature, although feminists have engaged in varying degrees with historical materialism.

the situation of women in his development of Marxist theory. Beauvoir contests his claim that women's oppression is related to the ownership of private property (*SS*: 86–89). She argues that, because human consciousness includes the 'original category of the Other and an original aspiration to dominate the Other', women's oppression ensued in the division of labour between the sexes (*SS*: 89). Engels does not account for the specificity of women's oppression, in Beauvoir's view; woman is not simply a worker, but a human being who has productive and reproductive capacities. Yet 'she is for man a sexual partner, a reproducer, an erotic object – an Other through whom he seeks himself' (*SS*: 90). In this sense, man seeks to possess woman and ends only in alienating himself in her. Beauvoir adopts a Marxist notion of productive activity as being crucial for human beings to transcend their animal nature (for information on Marxism, see Chapter 1, p. 18). She examines how women become alienated because they are marginalised from the workforce and society and reduced to their reproductive role. Woman alienates herself in man as absolute subject who can assume responsibility for her life. In this way, she adapts the Marxist notion of alienation to describe the situation of both women and men. Women, however, are socially alienated and corporeally alienated. In other words, women become objectified through their marginalisation from conscious productive activity (i.e. work) and through their relationship to their embodiment, experienced in patriarchal society.

This Marxist influence is discernible, as already noted, in Part II of *The Second Sex*, which is devoted to history – a section of the work regrettably abridged in the English edited translation. Ranging from the nomadic period to the 1940s, Beauvoir emphasises the importance of woman's role as absolute Other (see pp. 54–55), the advent of private property and woman's participation in production as being crucial to her situation. She also seeks to examine the role of women in history or, rather, the absence of women in historical accounts, again an aspect of *The Second Sex* which anticipates later work by feminist historians from the 1970s onwards.

Another important section of the first volume is the third part, which focuses on myths, or how gender is imagined and represented. As a writer, Beauvoir recognises that cultural representation acts as a powerful political force because it constitutes how a society imagines and represents itself to itself. In the context of gender relations, cultural forms such as literature and film can challenge or confirm sexist stereotyping of women and men. As we saw in Chapter 2, Beauvoir uses the example of Brigitte Bardot in French cinema of the 1950s to analyse how the myth of the 'eternal feminine' was revived. Beauvoir's concept of myth is rooted in part in the Marxist notion of ideology as 'false consciousness', or beliefs which conceal the economic basis of society and the oppression wreaked by capitalism. She also draws on both the analysis of mythical beliefs concerning the material world by the French philosopher of science and literary critic, Gaston Bachelard (1884–1962), and on the concept of myth in Claude Lévi-Strauss's *The Elementary Structures of Kinship*, which she read just before finishing *The Second Sex*. In turn, she also anticipates aspects of the ideological analysis of myth by Roland Barthes in his influential *Mythologies* (1957).

In this third section, Beauvoir examines myths of femininity and the purposes they serve. She focuses on myth as a response to the existential predicament of life itself, with its anguished recognition of the responsibility of freedom and the existence of the Other. She also traces myths of femininity at work in the literary texts of five male authors – Henry de Montherlant (1896–1972), D. H. Lawrence (1885–1930), Paul Claudel (1868–1955), André Breton (1896–1966), and Stendhal (alias Henri Beyle, 1783–1842) – to see how patriarchal ideology is perpetuated or challenged in cultural forms. Only one of these writers, the Romantic idealist Stendhal, comes close to representing woman as a transcendent being; although, for all of these writers, 'the ideal

ROLAND BARTHES (1915–1980)

Roland Barthes is known as a semiologist (an analyst of signs), a literary theorist and a structuralist, although he is difficult to classify. His main concern was with language, signs and literature and their interrelationships, which he explored in a range of influential books and essays, including *Mythologies* (1957) and *The Pleasure of the Text* (1973). From the late 1950s, he was associated with structuralism (see Chapter 5, p. 91) and with such notions as 'the death of the author' and the consequent pre-eminence of the critic. From the late 1960s, he focused more on subversive textuality and its pleasures.

woman will be she who incarnates most exactly the Other capable of revealing him to himself' (*SS*: 281).

LIVED EXPERIENCE

As noted earlier, the second volume of *The Second Sex* opens with the famous phrase: 'one is not born, but rather becomes, a woman'. In this volume, Beauvoir concentrates on what she calls women's 'lived experience'. She traces the lifecourse of women from infancy through to old age and demonstrates how sexually differentiated roles are learned from earliest infancy.

In her first chapter on 'childhood', Beauvoir draws on a range of psychoanalytic theory to describe male and female psychosexual development – for example, Havelock Ellis's *Studies in the Psychology of Sex* (1897–1928) and Helene Deutsch's *The Psychology of Women* (1944). She also refers to an early essay by the Freudian revisionist, Jacques Lacan (1901–1981), entitled 'Les Complexes familiaux dans la formation de l'individu' (1938), indicating her awareness of his developing and influential theory of alienation of the ego in 'the Mirror Stage'.

In *The Second Sex*, Beauvoir describes how girls and boys are rewarded or punished explicitly or implicitly according to how successfully they conform to the desired models of heterosexual masculinity and femininity which perpetuate patriarchy. This suggests that Beauvoir was aware of the social construction of masculinity as well as of femininity, which makes her 1949 text an early (albeit very limited) precursor to more recent debates on masculinity. In the learning of gender roles, she argues that spatiality is a key feature in the child's experience of transcendent subjectivity. For example, before puberty transforms the girl's body, she is discouraged from assuming her physicality and appropriating space in the world, whereas boys are encouraged to be more active in taking up physical space, by climbing trees and engaging in aggressive or noisy sports and hobbies. In this way, the assumption of a gendered identity involves a gendered spatial experience (*SS*: 313).

In her portrayal of sexual relationships in *The Second Sex*, she offers a more positive account of lesbian sexuality than heterosexuality, although, viewed together, the inconsistencies between the two accounts suggest that Beauvoir had not developed a coherent theory of female sexuality in her account of gendered subjectivity. The chapter on 'The lesbian' closes the 'Formative years' section, which suggests that Beauvoir did not envisage lesbianism as a long-term option for women.

In her portrayal of heterosexual sex, Beauvoir represents the woman as passive, while her male partner is predatory and aggressive. The man expresses his active subjectivity in sex, whereas the woman is equated with passive viscosity, the object of desire rather than the sexual initiator or peer – a prisoner of either clitoral pleasure (which Beauvoir associates with juvenile independence) or vaginal pleasure (associated with men and motherhood). It is worth noting in this context that several critics have accused Beauvoir of over-valorisation of male sexuality in *The Second Sex*. More specifically, Michèle Le Doeuff and others have noted how Beauvoir sometimes reproduces elements of Sartre's misogynist metaphors and discourse, exemplified in *Being and Nothingness* by his descriptions of female sexuality as 'slimy', seeing as 'deflowering' and knowledge as 'penetration' (Le Doeuff 1989: 79–81; Lundgren-Gothlin 1996: 207–210; Moi 1994: 168). There is, indeed, not a very positive account of heterosexuality in *The Second Sex*, but this is because Beauvoir argues that, in patriarchal society, heterosexual sex is predisposed to be symbolic of wider gender inequalities and, hence, a conflict-laden encounter devoid of reciprocity. This is not inevitable if 'woman finds in the male both desire and respect; if he lusts after her flesh while recognising her freedom [. . .] her integrity remains unimpaired [. . .] she remains free in the submission to which she consents' (*SS*: 421–422).

Beauvoir's account of lesbianism, however, is surprisingly radical for its time, for she notes that, within a patriarchal society, a lesbian relationship is at least as valid as any heterosexual relationship. Consistent with her existentialism, she argues that one is neither irrevocably heterosexual nor homosexual; one chooses one's sexuality perpetually and what is more pertinent is the authenticity of the choice. Beauvoir argues that all women are predisposed – in a somewhat 'adolescent' way – to have a physical affinity with women. This notion of a continuum of sexuality is radical for its time and had been used in the American sexologist Alfred Kinsey's influential *Sexual Behaviour in the Human Male* (1948) and *Sexual Behaviour in the Human Female* (1953) and was later used by the feminist theorist and poet Adrienne Rich in her influential 1980 essay, 'Compulsory heterosexuality and lesbian existence'. Beauvoir nevertheless marginalises lesbian experience in *The Second Sex* as a whole by confining her discussion largely to this single chapter and a few pages in 'The young girl'. She also makes no sustained attempt to address the issue of heterosexuality as a political institution in *The Second Sex*. Beauvoir appears to assume here that most women are irrevocably heterosexual. Moi has noted that she presents a confused picture of lesbianism, arguing both for its authenticity, but also that it is a narcissistic choice (Moi 1994: 199–203). Beauvoir appears to see lesbian sexuality both as a solipsistic attempt to recreate oneself and as a reciprocal sexual experience, unlike the conflict-laden heterosexual encounter. She does not consider the social, historical and political significance of assuming a lesbian identity in a traditionally homophobic and patriarchal society (Ferguson in Al-Hibri and Simons 1990: 285).

To summarise, sexuality is described in *The Second Sex* either as a conflict-laden exchange between an active male and passive female, who are both prisoners of naturalising biological mythology, or as a potentially reciprocal, yet rather narcissistic, exchange between women with no historical or political importance.

Unsurprisingly, Beauvoir does not view marriage or motherhood as happy experiences for women in patriarchal society. She argues in Part V that marriage has been promoted as the desirable norm, even though it has traditionally served male interests. Women also have little control over their experiences of motherhood as (in France in 1949) contraception and abortion are not freely available to them (*SS*: 502–510). For Beauvoir, there is no such thing as a maternal instinct

– it is a patriarchal fabrication which can instil maternal guilt because women's reactions to their motherhood are very variable: 'no maternal "instinct exists" [. . .] the mother's attitude depends on her total situation and her reaction to it' (*SS*: 526). She contends that motherhood is too important a task to entrust to a sector of the population who are denied full autonomy, because women, men and children suffer from the oppression of women.

An important point to remember about Beauvoir's analysis of women's situation in *The Second Sex* is that she does not hold men uniquely responsible for the oppression of women: patriarchal ideology only seems to 'work' because some women accept inauthentic roles determined for them by patriarchal ideology. Beauvoir deals with three inauthentic responses by women to their situation in the chapters on 'The narcissist', 'The woman in love' and 'The mystic' in Part VI, analysing ways in which women can be compliant with the mechanisms of their own oppression.

In the last part of her study, she examines the difficulties faced by women who try to live autonomously, their behaviour often judged by sexual and professional double standards:

> the independent woman of today is torn between her professional interests and the problems of her sexual life; it is difficult for her to strike a balance between the two; if she does, it is at the price of concessions and sacrifices which require her to be in a constant state of tension.
>
> (*SS*: 705)

Freedom is difficult for women because they are not used to assuming full responsibility in society and they therefore lack the patronage and experience from which men benefit. To exist autonomously, Beauvoir argues that women should not content themselves with easy answers, such as marriage and pregnancy, by which patriarchal society can trap them into relinquishing their claims to contribute independently and authentically to society. Her 'solution' is that women must strive to become economically independent and work together to gain a political analysis of their situation so they can challenge it. She also believed in 1949 that many of women's problems would be resolved by a socialist development of society – a position she later modified in the 1970s when she became active in the second-wave feminist struggle in France (see Chapter 4).

Despite its many inconsistencies, *The Second Sex* has been highly influential and remains deeply relevant to contemporary society in its concerns. Analysing the concept of woman as the 'absolute Other', the object of the male gaze, who is encouraged to alienate herself in her reproductive capacity, Beauvoir analyses the production and perpetuation of naturalising discourses of sexual difference. Her focus on the potentially fluid dynamics of power between the genders renders her study very modern.

In *The Second Sex* Beauvoir attempts to demonstrate the 'ambiguity' of women's situation and to challenge deterministic patriarchal discourses governing women's subjectivity. She has been accused of devaluing feminine activities and experience, but, as we noted at the start of this chapter, in post-war France, traditionally feminine spheres of activity were already over-valued – a situation which she attempted to challenge. The key issue for Beauvoir in *The Second Sex* was to articulate how women might become transcendent, authentic subjects in their own right.

SUMMARY

Drawing on a synthesis of existential phenomenology, Marxism, ethics and anthropology, Beauvoir provides an ethical analysis of woman's existence and situation in *The Second Sex*. She argues that woman has been positioned as the 'absolute Other' to man's role as universal transcendent subject. There is, according to Beauvoir, no 'natural' femininity or masculinity or any maternal 'instinct'. Woman 'becomes' her gender by learning to conform to patriarchal society's requirements that she exist inauthentically – for example, as a passive body for consumption by the male gaze and by abandoning her freedom and devoting herself to the roles of wife and mother. Beauvoir says that woman, like man, is (potentially) a morally free being who is responsible for her own life. To achieve their freedom, women must become economically independent and politically aware of their situation collectively. Authentic relations between women and men depend on their recognition of each other as morally free subjects for the ultimate benefit of all humanity.

4

FEMINIST PRAXIS

Despite the fact that Simone de Beauvoir wrote *The Second Sex* in the mid 1940s, she did not call herself a feminist until 1965. This was because she rejected 'first-wave' feminist groups in France prior to the MLF as reformist and insufficiently radical in their political projects. In 1970, she was asked by activists to become involved in second-wave feminist campaigns, such as the fight for legalised abortion. The 1970s then became a period of feminist activism for Beauvoir. But how did she connect the feminist theory of *The Second Sex* with feminist praxis?

It will be the purpose of this chapter to represent the development of Beauvoir's feminist thought as it developed after *The Second Sex*, both prior to and during the second-wave feminist movement in France. She did not write a sequel to *The Second Sex* and so her thought in this period

PRAXIS

'Praxis' is a Marxist term meaning the unity of theory and practice in a bid to change simultaneously oneself and society. In *The German Ideology* (1845–1846), Marx says that 'the coincidence of the changing of circumstances and of human activity or self-changing can be conceived and rationally understood only as revolutionary practice' (Marx 1977: 156).

was articulated mainly in interviews – which can themselves be considered as a mode of thought – and in short texts. First, however, we need to examine briefly the initial impact of Beauvoir's ground-breaking work on gender.

RECEPTION OF *THE SECOND SEX* 1949–1970

On its publication in 1949, the first volume of *The Second Sex* sold 22,000 copies: it was a 'succès de scandale'. But, as noted in Chapter 3, it was published in a deeply traditional France, still marked by the effects of misogynist Vichy ideology and the German Occupation. The Catholic Church and the Communist Party, who both opposed sexual liberation and contraception, were powerful influences in French people's lives. As noted earlier, women had only just won the right to vote (1944), abortion and contraception were illegal and women could not work without their husband's consent. For many, shocked by Beauvoir's open discussion of sexuality, *The Second Sex* was considered indecent and outrageous. Camus even accused Beauvoir of 'making the French male look ridiculous' (*FC*: 200). Despite the furore, the political impact of the text was only gradual, until it was read by second-wave French feminists and, following its edited translation into English in 1953, Anglo-American feminists, such as Betty Friedan (*The Feminine Mystique*, 1963), Kate Millett (*Sexual Politics*, 1970), Germaine Greer (*The Female Eunuch*, 1970) and Juliet Mitchell (*Psychoanalysis and Feminism*, 1974). Although there are few, if any, explicit references to *The Second Sex* in these works, it was nevertheless important in establishing their subsequent arguments for women's liberation.

In the 1950s and early 1960s in France, the muted reception of *The Second Sex* meant that it was mainly summarised in critical works devoted to Beauvoir's writing. It was not yet read as a work of feminist philosophy. In Geneviève Gennari's 1958 study, *Simone de Beauvoir* (the first critical examination of her writing), the arguments of *The Second Sex* are cautiously welcomed, although Gennari rejects Beauvoir's notion that a maternal instinct does not exist and advocates a biologically deterministic view of gender roles. In 1969, the Belgian novelist and literary critic, Suzanne Lilar, launched an in-depth attack on *The Second Sex* – the first to engage with Beauvoir's text in detail – accusing her of ignoring sexual difference, and of disregarding female nature and maternal instinct (Lilar 1969). Lilar argued instead that biology and sexual identity were crucial determining factors in the intrinsic bisexuality of women and men. Beauvoir did not respond, recognising perhaps that Lilar's arguments were rooted in the very naturalistic and essentialising gender discourses which she had attempted to challenge in *The Second Sex*. Lilar's attack on *The Second Sex* anticipated French differentialist feminism's rejection of Beauvoir's materialist feminism later in the 1970s. As we have seen in Chapter 3, she does not deny the existence of biological differences between women and men, but argues that these differences are (1) not 'natural facts', but *culturally* determined, and (2) inadequate to justify the oppression of women.

BEAUVOIR: 'JE SUIS RADICALEMENT FEMINISTE'

Prior to the eruption of second-wave feminism in France, Beauvoir participated in two important interviews in 1965 with Francis Jeanson and talked about her feminism and women's condition (Jeanson 1966: 251–298). Jeanson, a supporter of *The Second Sex*, had worked with Sartre and Beauvoir at *Les Temps Modernes* and initiated their involvement in support of the Front de Libération Nationale (FLN), the movement fighting for Algerian independence from France, during the Algerian War (1954–1962). Beauvoir explains in these interviews her notion of sexual difference as being a 'cultural fact' which, as a result of the way in which society is organised, is constituted as a major social difference. For the first time, Beauvoir declares herself 'radicalement féministe' ('completely feminist') in that she fundamentally discounts the determining importance of sexual difference (Jeanson 1966: 258). She also laments the fact that psychoanalysis in the 1960s was still claiming that girls experienced 'penis envy'. Beauvoir questions here whether women's erotic desire is so different from that of men and whether there are just as many differences in the experience of erotic desire among men as among women. Beauvoir emphasises that, although she recognises differences between men and women as social groups in contemporary society, she does not recognise any essential difference between individual women and men. She condemns antagonistic relationships between women and men, but questions why women and men live together in such conditions. She agrees with Jeanson that, in the mid 1960s, gender relations are undergoing a period of transition.

Beauvoir notes that motherhood might be a positive experience, although she does not fundamentally differentiate it from fatherhood. Observing a child's development would hold much more interest for her now than it did when she wrote *The Second Sex* because she had become more interested in psychoanalysis (Jeanson 1966: 283). She also notes that fatherhood might be just as interesting an experience as motherhood, although cultural rather than biological factors, in her view, encourage maternal narcissism relating to pregnancy and labour. She says that she would defend *The Second Sex* at all costs, among her published works.

After the onset of second-wave feminism in France, Beauvoir became involved in a variety of ways in the feminist struggle, but, before we look at her thinking during this period, it is necessary to outline the main axes of feminist struggle in France in the 1970s.

FRENCH FEMINISM IN THE 1970S

The 'big bang' for second-wave French feminism came with the May 1968 'événements'. This crisis in French society was initially a student assault on the university system, but rapidly became a much wider political crisis as striking workers in industry and commerce brought the country to a standstill. De Gaulle's presidency of France initially survived the crisis (although he resigned the following year) and 'May '68' resulted in a weakened French Communist Party, vigorous ideological debate on the Left and a right-wing backlash in the 1969 general elections. A feature of political organisation during the 'May '68' period and its aftermath was a rejection of hierarchical forms of organisation and of conventional party politics as a way of revolution-ising French society. Politics became more pluralist and open to feminism, the Third World and environmentalism. But women activists realised quickly that any feminist revolution would not be instigated by male-dominated, radical left-wing groups because, there also, women were still confined to their traditional roles, servicing male activists who did not or would not recognise that 'the personal is political' (Duchen 1986: 6–8, 44). The MLF emerged as a spontaneous collec-tion of diverse groupings, many of which rejected formal organisation and hierarchy. Three broad tendencies came into existence. One of these was a materialist grouping, inspired by, but not aligned to,

Marxism, which prioritised women's struggle against patriarchy. Another grouping, rooted in French socialism, prioritised women's solidarity with the working class to fight capitalism (known as the 'tendance lutte des classes' or class struggle tendency) and a third grouping, 'Psychanalyse et politique', which advocated the existence of a repressed female difference which would emerge once 'phallocratic' society had been dismantled. 'Psych et po' (as it was known) declared itself to be opposed to feminism, seeing in it a reformist attempt to replace men with women in society without dismantling the patriarchal discursive order.

One of the successes of the post-1968 feminist period was the campaign for abortion, which was conducted through rallies and high-profile political actions, such as the 'Manifeste des 343', which Beauvoir signed. This was published by the left-wing weekly news magazine, *Le Nouvel Observateur*, and in the left-of-centre daily broadsheet, *Le Monde*, on 5 April 1971, as a manifesto declaring that 343 activists, film stars, writers and public figures had broken the law and had had an abortion. Then, in 1972, Beauvoir set up 'Choisir', a campaign group for free contraception and abortion, with writer, Christiane Rochefort, actress, Delphine Seyrig, and lawyer, Gisèle Halimi. Beauvoir had already worked with Halimi in 1960 during the Algerian War to defend Djamila Boupacha, a 23-year-old Algerian woman, who had been accused of spying, then tortured and raped by French soldiers. Beauvoir also testified at the 1972 landmark 'Bobigny trial' for a 17-year-old girl accused of having had an illegal abortion. The campaign to legalise abortion resulted in its legalisation in 1974 in the first ten weeks of pregnancy for a trial period of five years and, in 1979, the law was given permanent status.

Meanwhile, other actions took place in the early 1970s, such as the 1972 rally in Paris denouncing crimes against women. This drew over 5,000 women, some of whom testified to their experiences of male violence, sexuality and motherhood. Rape crisis centres and women's refuges were set up as well as feminist newspapers and journals in which feminist political ideas were debated. Yet the MLF was not a cohesive, homogeneous movement. There were deeply-rooted fundamental differences between factions, such as 'Psych et po' and radical materialist feminists, over notions of gender identity and women's situation in society more generally. These ideological differences fell broadly into three areas: the relation of women's struggle to the class struggle and the roots of women's oppression more generally; the existence (or not) of sexual difference; and, finally, the relative merits of hetero-sexuality and lesbianism as political strategies in patriarchal society (Duchen 1986: 18–25). By the mid 1970s, the MLF was increasingly fragmented, particularly after the success of the abortion campaign, and, in 1979, in a reactionary move, the 'Psych et po' tendency appropriated the MLF name as their trademark and registered the MLF as their company property.

The rift between sexual differentialist and materialist feminisms was manifest in women's literary and theoretical writing from the 1970s onwards. During the 1970s, and into the early 1980s, there was a proliferation both of realist, testimonial literature by women exploring their lives and of avant-garde texts which sought to explore women's psychosocial difference through experimental attempts to write the body in 'écriture féminine' (see Chapter 5). Theoretical writings by figures such as Hélène Cixous, Luce Irigaray and Julia Kristeva sought to theorise in their individually different ways how the feminine and the maternal might be rethought through a subversion of language and existing systems of thought in order to reject patriarchal notions of woman as 'Other'. As Duchen has argued, it was viewed 'as important to dismantle the givens of phallogocentric discourse as it [was] to demystify the structures of patriarchy' (Duchen 1986: 84).

Beauvoir was theoretically closest to the materialist feminist tendency in France during this period. She firmly rejected differen-tialist feminism because, as she had demonstrated in The Second Sex, discourses of 'sexual difference' had traditionally been exploited by patriarchy to oppress women. She viewed differentialist feminism as espousing an ideology of neo-femininity which was politically regres-sive. Consequently, she continued to reject any recourse to notions of repressed female difference as an effective political strategy to combat women's oppression. Beauvoir's analysis of gender continued to be resolutely anti-naturalist, seeing any reference to woman's 'nature' or to woman's maternal vocation as anathema to women's liberation and autonomy. She was also critical of what she saw as the elitism of differentialist theorists, such as Hélène Cixous, whose esoteric work was not readily accessible to the average woman (Beauvoir 1979b: 229–230).

BEAUVOIR'S FEMINISM IN THE 1970s AND 1980s

Beauvoir participated in a major series of interviews between 1972 and 1982 with Alice Schwarzer, a German feminist, which are of interest here to our examination of the development of her feminist thought (Beauvoir 1984). Schwarzer interviewed Beauvoir initially both to publicise what she termed Beauvoir's 'conversion' to feminism and to raise money for the MLF. In the first interview, Beauvoir explains that she joined an MLF demonstration in November 1971 for the right to abortion on demand and free contraception because she realised that, since the publication of *The Second Sex*, women's situation had not really improved. Condemning the reformist and legalistic aspects of women's groups prior to the MLF, Beauvoir explains that she was attracted to the radical nature of post-1968 materialist feminism. Recognising the political limitations of her statement at the end of *The Second Sex* that women's situation would improve in the context of socialist development, Beauvoir here crucially advocates a specific struggle, on the part of women and men, linked to the class struggle, to fight for women's equality. She accepts the temporary exclusion of men from the political process on the grounds that women have to analyse their own specific oppression apart from men and also because, even if men are also in certain ways victims of the patriarchal system, they nevertheless profit from it and internalise its ideology.

Beauvoir claims in this first interview with Schwarzer in 1972 not to have thought about the value of lesbianism as a political strategy (this was an important question for second-wave feminism) and contests the notion that all heterosexual relations are necessarily oppressive. As in *The Second Sex*, Beauvoir advocates that paid work is the necessary precondition for women's independence and that women must organise themselves collectively to achieve their autonomy. She accepts the limited use of violence in self-defence so that women can counter male aggression.

Schwarzer interviewed Beauvoir again in 1976, shortly after abortion has been legalised. Despite its advantages, Beauvoir warns against the potential backlash of 'free abortion' in that she anticipates that it can be used against women as a means to pressurise them into having sex. She claims here to have been radicalised in many of her views by younger feminists in the MLF and to have learnt the importance of political vigilance. Here, Beauvoir comments on a range of current debates in feminist politics, rejecting, for example, wages for domestic work on the grounds that domestic responsibility should be shared by everyone. Here, she accepts lesbianism as a temporary political strategy, although claims that, in itself, homosexuality is just as limiting as heterosexuality – nevertheless, this constitutes a development in Beauvoir's thinking on lesbianism compared to her views expressed in *The Second Sex* and in the 1972 interview with Schwarzer.

The fourth interview with Schwarzer took place on Beauvoir's seventieth birthday in 1978. In this interview she explains that she would like to have given a frank and balanced account of her sexuality in her memoirs and says that she did not realise that sexuality, particularly the autobiographical representation of her own sexuality, was such an important question. She implicitly recognises here the importance of consciousness-raising and the political significance of her own life story. She also comments on her interest in feminist psychoanalysis, saying that, if she were much younger, she would write a feminist study of psychoanalysis, alluding to the feminist theorist and psychoanalyst Luce Irigaray's *Speculum, of the Other Woman* (1974) and *This Sex Which Is Not One* (1977). In 1977, Beauvoir had commented on her interest in Irigaray's work, although complaining about what she saw as the laborious Lacanian style of *Speculum* and the lack of audacity in her critique of Freudian psychoanalysis (Beauvoir 1979b: 228).

In 1980 and 1982, in further interviews with Schwarzer, Beauvoir discusses her collaborative working relationship with Sartre, saying that they worked together in developing various philosophical questions but that she opposed his ideas on freedom, instead arguing for the importance of 'situation' – a view which Sartre subsequently accepted. Beauvoir also denies having had sexual involvements with women – an inaccurate response which can be explained by her recognition in the 1978 Schwarzer interview that speaking honestly about her sexual life would be impossible now as it would implicate people who are close to her. Lastly, Beauvoir rejects the emergence of 'new femininity' and the mystification of motherhood. Asked if feminism has failed, she says that it has only reached a small number of women, although certain mass campaigns, such as the fight for abortion, have reached much larger groups of people who perceive feminism as an ideological threat.

The Schwarzer interviews are important because they enable us to see the evolution of Beauvoir's thinking on women's situation not only in terms of those expressed in *The Second Sex*, but also in terms of her contact with younger feminists throughout the 1970s. Beauvoir's feminist activism threw her into the heart of feminist debates and campaigns in the 1970s and caused her to modify some of her views, for example, on sexuality. In this way, the theories propounded in *The Second Sex* slowly became feminist praxis.

In an interview with John Gerassi in 1975, Beauvoir comments further on the impact of *The Second Sex* and her feminism (Beauvoir 1976: 79–85). Here, she rejects the suggestion that her study of women constituted the beginning of second-wave feminism, especially in the United States, because the majority of feminist activists would have been too young to have been influenced by it (Beauvoir 1976: 79). This is rather modest claim on Beauvoir's part, for US feminists, such as Kate Millett, do recognise *The Second Sex* as a major influence on their work. In this interview Beauvoir describes her own life as being exceptional in the sense that, as a middle-class intellectual, she benefited from having choices and opportunities denied to working-class women. She argues that sexism is equally present in left-wing organisations as elsewhere in patriarchal society; consequently, feminism's fight for sexual equality has to take place independently of the class struggle (Beauvoir 1976: 80). She now rejects the proposition that a socialist revolution would achieve sexual equality because patriarchal values remain unchallenged in so-called socialist countries such as the Soviet Union and Czechoslovakia. She sees the recognition that socialism will not bring sexual equality as one of the most important developments of second-wave feminism.

Beauvoir argues that a feminist is, by definition, left-wing, because she is fighting for total equality – social equality is implied in the fight for sexual equality (Beauvoir 1976: 81). She also defends feminist separatism and the use of consciousness-raising groups for women to discover their identity as women. She likens lesbian separatism as a political strategy (rather than uniquely on the basis of sexual orientation) to the black power movement in the United States. However, radical lesbian separatists, in her experience, also show solidarity with other political struggles (Beauvoir 1976: 83).

Beauvoir argues here that feminist progress can only be effected by a combination of new laws favouring women's emancipation (such as the 1975 Veil law on abortion) accompanied by mass political campaigns (Beauvoir 1976: 84). Finally, she says that, if she were to write a sequel to *The Second Sex*, it would have to be a collective project, based on praxis rather than theory. In her view, all revolutionary struggles should develop their theory from praxis (Beauvoir 1976: 84). This is a crucial admission on Beauvoir's part, indicating her political development since the late 1940s, because now she advocates the importance of direct political action as a prerequisite to political theory.

In 1973, Beauvoir's belief in the importance of analysing the effects of patriarchal power in everyday circumstances informed the decision to set up a column in *Les Temps Modernes* devoted to 'everyday sexism'. This initiative aimed to expose discriminatory behaviour and language directed at women which, unlike racial discrimination, passed unsanctioned by the courts (Francis and Gontier 1979: 514). For example, it was illegal to speak or write in a derogatory way about Jews or black people, but entirely legal to refer to women in derogatory ways in print or in speech. This everyday sexism was extremely widespread and was exposed in *Les Temps Modernes*. A year later, in 1974, Beauvoir was also made director of the League for Women's Rights which, among other issues, was concerned with fighting for battered women.

Beauvoir then became editorial director of *Questions Féministes* (later *Nouvelles Questions Féministes*), a radical feminist journal launched in 1977. Its original collective included Christine Delphy, who became one of the main exponents of French materialist feminism, and later it included the radical feminist theorist and writer, Monique Wittig. Although Beauvoir was not closely involved with the journal at a day-to-day level, her support was consistent with her feminist politics. *Questions Féministes* approached women's oppression from a materialist perspective and was 'dedicated to the analysis of patriarchy as a social system in which women and men constitute different classes with opposing interests' (Jackson 1996: 22).

Questions Féministes existed for approximately three years before it was dissolved in the context of a major political rift within the MLF more generally, concerning the relationship between lesbianism and feminism (Duchen 1986: 22–25). The terms of this debate within *Questions Féministes* and the MLF more generally were not specific to France, for the issue of how to pursue a radical feminist agenda and maintain personal and economic relationships with men divided radical feminists in Britain and elsewhere (Jackson 1996: 23). *Nouvelles Questions Féministes* was launched by Delphy (to replace *Questions Féministes*) and again supported by Beauvoir as titular editor, who

WOMEN AS A 'CLASS'

The notion that women and men constitute opposing classes is fundamental to French radical feminism, especially to the work of Christine
Delphy (Jackson 1996: 92–114). Feminist theorists outside France (for
example, Canadian radical feminist, Shulamith Firestone, in *The Dialectic of
Sex* in 1972) have also conceptualised women as a class, on the basis of relations of reproduction and sexuality.

condemned the radical lesbian position of Wittig and her supporters,
accusing them of excluding heterosexual women from the class of
women.

In 1978, Beauvoir seized another opportunity to publicise her
feminism, thirty years after *The Second Sex*, in an interview with the
daily newspaper, *Le Monde*. Here she still holds to her original notion
that femininity and masculinity are social constructions (Beauvoir
1979c: 583). Women's situation had deteriorated in the late 1970s
because of increased male hostility to women's liberation. The new
abortion law was not being sufficiently enforced, for illegal abortions
were still widespread. Beauvoir recognises that new careers are
opening up for women, but identifies the existence of a glass ceiling
in the jobs market which prevents women from reaching top jobs.
She argues that, although certain professions, such as law, teaching
and medicine, have become more feminised, they are simultaneously
devalued or women remain segregated in certain lower prestige areas
of the professions, hence the greater numbers of women working in
paediatric medicine and midwifery (Beauvoir 1979c: 587). The next
issues for women to tackle in fighting sexual discrimination are equal
salaries for equal work and the sharing of domestic labour. She
continues to have little faith in the mainstream political parties in
France who, in her view, are unconcerned with women's issues. She
doubts whether more women in French politics would do much to
improve women's condition because it would be necessary to change
the way political power is exercised and to reject patriarchal political
values. In Beauvoir's view, the modest improvement in women's
situation over the last twenty-five years is due to feminism rather
than socialism, which has largely failed in its mission (Beauvoir 1979c:
589).

Beauvoir continued to support feminist struggle in the later years of her life until her death in 1986. She also wrote prefatory texts to publicise other political and moral issues, for example to the screenplay of Claude Lanzmann's documentary about the Holocaust, *Shoah* (1985) and to an AIDS testimony, *Mihloud* (1986). Since the 1970s, feminist thinkers across the disciplines have continued to engage with her work and Beauvoir's impact on these thinkers will be the focus of the final chapter.

SUMMARY

Despite the initial furore on its publication in the 1950s and 1960s, Beauvoir's *The Second Sex* met with a muted political reaction. Following the appearance of the edited English translation in 1953, Anglo-American feminists, such as Friedan, Millett, Greer and Firestone, began to engage with Beauvoir's ideas. In France, in the late 1960s, differentialist feminists began to contest the anti-naturalism of her arguments. During the 'second wave' of French feminism after 1968, Beauvoir supported materialist feminists and worked with them on issues such as abortion, violence against women and women's rights more generally. In the 1970s, she did not recount any of her original arguments in *The Second Sex*, although she now recognised that socialism would not incorporate a feminist revolution of society. She also acknowledged that she had underestimated the political significance of women's sexuality. She recognised that deriving political praxis from theoretical works such as *The Second Sex* was no longer valid; in all political struggles, theory should now be derived from collective praxis.

5

LITERATURE

So far we have looked at some of Beauvoir's key philosophical ideas; the purpose of this chapter will be to acquaint ourselves with some of her key ideas about literature. Now, as indicated at the beginning of this book, literary and philosophical concerns are not easy to separate in her writing. Working in both disciplines, Beauvoir cites literary examples in her philosophical writing and draws on her philosophical knowledge in her literary writing. She explained in a 1985 interview that 'I'm infused with philosophy and when I put philosophy into my books it's because that's a way for me to view the world' (Beauvoir in Simons 1999: 93). In this way, philosophy infuses many of her literary and political concerns.

LITERATURE AND METAPHYSICS

Beauvoir's interest in working at the border crossing of literature and philosophy is evident in one of her earliest texts about literature: 'Littérature et métaphysique', published in *Les Temps Modernes* in 1946. In this essay, she defends the metaphysical novel and the various generic forms exploited by existentialism.

Beauvoir shared these preoccupations with her contemporary, Maurice Merleau-Ponty who, in a review of Beauvoir's first published novel, *She Came to Stay*, in 1948, discusses the text as a philosophical novel, but also makes some general statements about the relationship

METAPHYSICS

This is a broad area of philosophy, closely related to ontology, comprising two main strands of enquiry into (1) the nature of reality, and (2) what is real, which are separate from the terms in which that reality might be described.

between literature and philosophy. In 'Metaphysics and the novel', he argues that links between literature and philosophy have been getting closer since the end of the nineteenth century, giving way to 'hybrid modes of expression having elements of the intimate diary, the philosophical treatise and the dialogue' (Merleau-Ponty 1964: 27). He notes that literature, philosophy and politics are different expressions of a certain attitude towards the world expressed in intellectual works. This attitude is not specific to existentialism since, prior to the introduction of existentialist philosophy in France, life had already been defined as 'latent metaphysics' and metaphysics as 'an explicitation of human life'. He says that 'the tasks of literature and philosophy can no longer be separated' and asserts that Beauvoir's *She Came to Stay* signifies 'the development of a metaphysical literature and the end of a moral literature' (Merleau-Ponty 1964: 28). The British philosopher and writer, Iris Murdoch (1919–1999), interprets Merleau-Ponty's assertion as a recognition that 'in an existentialist novel the interest is focused upon the ambiguity of the characters' situation and upon how the characters choose to resolve this' (Murdoch 1999: 188)

In Beauvoir's essay, 'Littérature et métaphysique', she initially recognises that attempts to reconcile literary and philosophical modes of engagement with the world have a long history. She notes that the meaning of a novel cannot be reduced to simple formulae – that would be a betrayal of the writer's freedom and choice of genre. Whereas a philosopher provides an intellectual reconstruction of experience, a novelist represents that experience on an imaginary plane. She explains that metaphysics is not a system, but an attitude adopted by a human being who, in her totality, encounters the totality of the world (*LM*: 97). A metaphysical apprehension of the world is experienced by most people at some point in their lives. If you find yourself wondering about the meaning of life and the 'bigger picture', you are having metaphysical thoughts!

The universal significance of this metaphysical reality can be elucidated in abstract language in an atemporal and objective system: this is what we might term pure philosophy. When philosophers such as Hegel and Kierkegaard have wanted to emphasise the role and value of subjective experience, they have drawn on literary and biblical myths. We can also note this use of literary examples by Beauvoir in *The Second Sex* and in *Old Age*, where she draws on a wide range of writers to illustrate her arguments. The novel, on the other hand, represents the concrete singularity of experience in all its ambiguity. In the novel, reality is shown as a living synthesis between action and emotion before becoming thought (*LM*: 101)

Beauvoir explains that existentialist thought is consequently expressed both in philosophical treatises and in fiction because it aims to reconcile the subjective and objective, the absolute and the relative, the atemporal and the historical aspects of reality. Existentialism claims to seize the essence at the heart of existence (*LM*: 100).

The metaphysical novel, at its best, honestly engaged with by both writer and reader, represents human beings and events in their relation with the totality of the world. Beauvoir sees the reader as having a crucial role to play in participating in the creation of the imaginary world proposed by the author (*LM*: 103). The reader should not avoid this risk of imaginative engagement by substituting their own agenda, for the task of the novel is to appeal to the reader's freedom (*LM*: 104). In Beauvoir's view, it achieves what pure philosophy and pure literature cannot, namely the representation of the living unity and fundamental ambiguity of our human destiny within both its historical and eternal dimensions (*LM*: 104–105).

'Littérature et métaphysique' is an important and early statement of her views about the relationship between fiction and philosophy and helps us to understand what has been termed her 'literary-philosophical method' (Fullbrook and Fullbrook 1998: 43).

It has also been argued that this essay provides evidence of Beauvoir's critique of universalism in that she is arguing for the philosophical relevance of individual human experience (Fullbrook and Fullbrook 1998: 39). This is also evident in her philosophical essays, including *The Second Sex*, and in much of her fiction. In *Pyrrhus et Cinéas*, for example, as we have noted, Beauvoir addresses issues concerning situation, the relationship with the Other and the nature of action – issues which she would explore in a specific fictional context in the stories of Jean Blomart and Hélène Bertrand in *The Blood of Others*.

After what she characterised in *The Prime of Life* as the 'moral phase' of her literary career, Beauvoir did not write another explicit statement on her literary methods until the 1960s. In the meantime, she did, however, analyse myths of femininity in male literature in *The Second Sex* (see Part III of the first volume) as we saw in Chapter 3, and discuss her literary writing and interests in occasional interviews and in her four volumes of memoirs, published in France from 1958 onwards.

COMMITTED WRITING

From the 1940s, Beauvoir and Sartre were associated with a particular type of writing known as 'committed' or 'engaged' literature – the 'manifesto' of this literary movement being Sartre's *What is Literature?* (1948). In terms of Beauvoir's own textual practice, the term might generally be applied to her fictional writing from *The Blood of Others* onwards.

In *What is Literature?*, Sartre argues that the creative arts, but literature, in particular, are necessarily committed. All literature is rooted in and projects a world view, whether the writer acknowledges it or not and for which he or she must assume responsibility. This constitutes a mode of action in the world, according to Sartre. The text appeals to the freedom of the reader and opens up the writer's world view to the reader, who is challenged in the act of reading. Once the writer assumes responsibility for the moral and political significance of the world-view of the text, he or she can mobilise the influence of their work (its reception or how it is received by the reader) to struggle for a more socially just world. True to his notion of existentialist freedom, Sartre does not lay down any privileged course of action to achieve commitment, for we are each responsible for assuming our freedom and making our own choices.

This notion of literature has aesthetic and political implications for literary form and content, as is manifest in both Sartre and Beauvoir's literary practice from the 1940s: for example, they both reject the use of an omniscient narrator and 'zero focalisation' in favour of multiple internal and external focalisers. The reader, consequently, has no more information than any of the characters in the narrative and (in theory, at least) can engage imaginatively in the act of reading, rather than have

FOCALISATION

'Focalisation' (or 'point of view') is the perspective from which a story is viewed, and can change at any time during the course of the story. The focaliser may not be the same as the narrator (the person who relates the story). Three types of focalisation can be distinguished: 'zero focalisation', in which the reader has a bird's-eye view of everything in the story (including the characters' thoughts) and has access to more information than the characters involved; 'external focalisation', in which characters are selectively viewed from 'outside' with no access to their thoughts; and 'internal focalisation', in which the reader is plunged into a particular character's mind and, hence, has only a very partial perspective. Beauvoir frequently uses multiple narrator-focalisers, for example in *She Came to Stay* and *The Blood of Others*, and alternates external and internal focalisation, which enables her to represent characters as they exist for-others and for-themselves. Switching between internal and external focalisation is particularly effective in representing women's alienated situation in patriarchal society and is used very successfully in *Les Belles Images* (1966).

the omniscient author-narrator's world-view 'dictated' to her, thereby denying her freedom.

Beauvoir and Sartre also avoid typecast, predetermined characterisation in favour of 'situated' characters who are thrown into metaphysical dilemmas and who are obliged to confront their anguish resulting from an awareness of their freedom and choices. For example, in *The Blood of Others*, Beauvoir's second novel, Jean Blomart is 'situated' as a middle-class, politically aware character who, as a leader in the French Resistance, has to decide whether to sanction acts of sabotage against the Germans during the Second World War. Blomart has a keen sense of his responsibility for other people and knows that such acts will immediately meet with German reprisals against the French population. In existentialist terms, Blomart has to choose to act and assume his (relative) freedom and his ethical relationship to other people. His anguished decision to sanction the sabotage will necessarily impact negatively on those innocent people who will be killed in retaliation by the German troops, but, by sanctioning the sabotage, the German occupying forces are further weakened and an end to the war is in sight. Jean comes to accept, then, that the 'ends' in this particular situation are justified by the 'means' to achieve those ends.

There is also an emphasis on the phenomenological experience of time in *The Blood of Others*, as in other 'committed' literary texts. Most of the action of the story is told in flashback, enabling the reader to understand the sequence of events which led to Jean making his final decision to sanction the sabotage. Yet it also allows the reader to see how past, present and anticipated future events and experiences are interwoven in the choices made by the characters.

THE NEW NOVEL (OR 'NEW REALISM')

This development in French literature, mainly from the mid 1950s, is associated with Alain Robbe-Grillet (1922–), Nathalie Sarraute (1902–1999), Michel Butor (1926–), Claude Simon (1913–) and Robert Pinget (1919–1997) and sometimes with the early fiction of Marguerite Duras (1914–1996) and Samuel Beckett (1906–1989). Although there were significant disagreements between these writers concerning textual practice, there was a general consensus that character, story, commitment and the distinction between form and content should be rejected. The 'new novel' rejected any use of literature to communicate a political or socially committed message, emphasising instead its aesthetic function. It opposed a particular tradition of nineteenth-century humanistic realism, exemplified by the French novelist, Honoré de Balzac (1799–1850), which used well-defined characters, logical plot and a moral or political message in its reproduction of reality. The 'new novel' avoided the reproduction of a pre-existing 'reality' and focused instead on its own processes of construction, exposing the workings of language to subvert the conventions of writing. Although a typical 'new novel' does not exist, characteristics of such writing might be a minute attention to detail, non-linear narration of story, a confusion of what is 'real' and imagined, a rejection of traditional characterisation and, consequently, a challenge to the reader who is required to engage actively with the text to create meaning. Despite their public pronouncements, Sartre and Beauvoir did not oppose the 'new novel' completely (Jeanson 1966: 295). Sartre wrote a preface to Nathalie Sarraute's *Portrait d'un inconnu* (1947) and Beauvoir's *Les Belles Images* (1966) bears some traces of its characteristics (Beauvoir 1966 in Stefanson 1980: 56, 59).

TEL QUEL

Tel Quel was an influential avant-garde theoretical journal which first appeared in 1960. It initially enthusiastically supported the 'new novel' until the late 1960s, seeing in it a viable alternative to Sartrean commitment. It attracted major figures among its contributors, such as Roland Barthes (1915–1980), Georges Bataille (1897–1962), Jacques Derrida (1930–), Michel Foucault (1926–1984), Julia Kristeva (1941–), Philippe Sollers (1936–) and Jean Ricardou (1932–). Over the two decades of its existence, it engaged with linguistics, philosophy, psychoanalysis, Marxism, Maoism and theology in its theorisations of literature.

Through the 1950s and 1960s in France 'committed fiction' came under attack from the 'new novelists' and the *Tel Quel* group. Sartre and Beauvoir defended their notions of literature in response to these new literary developments.

LITERATURE IN THE 1960s

In December 1964, Beauvoir participated with Sartre in a debate between supporters of committed literature and partisans of the *Tel Quel* group, at this time close to the 'new novel'. The topic of the debate was the value and power of literature in the 1960s. Sartre had recently been interviewed by *Le Monde* and had talked at length about his disillusionment with literature in the face of material poverty, especially in the Third World. He had criticised his own early literature for being insufficiently aware of social inequality and implicitly criticised proponents of the 'new novel' as being actively reactionary.

On the 'committed' side of the debate were Beauvoir, Sartre and the Holocaust writer, Jorge Semprun (1923–), and on the *Tel Quel*/ 'new novel' side were the writers, Jean-Pierre Faye (1925–), Jean Ricardou (1932–) and Yves Berger (1934–). The main axis of the debate was the confrontation between Sartre and Ricardou, who was at the time the main proponent of the values of the 'new novel'. However, our focus here is Beauvoir's contribution to the debate and her defence of her vision of literature in the 1960s.

Beauvoir begins by asserting that the value of literature is to communicate the singularity of people's different situations: authentic literature transcends the separation between individuals (Beauvoir 1965: 79). Like Sartre, Beauvoir sees the author as presenting a world-view and a unique voice to the reader. But the writer cannot represent the world in a fixed image or represent the diverse complexity of the world: he or she can only represent a partial truth. So readers who believe in Balzac's realism are naive, in Beauvoir's view, for the author only ever represents a partial, constructed view of his or her world. She notes that the contemporary tendency for the reader to reject identification with characters is misplaced because, whether a novel has characters or not (she is implicitly referring to the 'new novel' here), the reader must still identify with someone (for example, the author or narrator) to be able to enter the world of the text and for the act of reading to be successful. The value of literature, in Beauvoir's view, is that it can transport the reader into the author's world, for it is a privileged locus of intersubjectivity.

However, literature must be authentic in that it must be rooted in a genuine quest on the part of the author, who must not know in advance what he or she is going to write. The form and content of a literary work are indivisible. Unsurprisingly, Beauvoir argues that the committed writer has the richest links with the world. In personal terms, she sees literature as being able to reconcile the irreconcilable moments of human experience, for words fight against time, death and separation. However, in her view, literature must deal with the failures and misery of the human condition, and not be hijacked by socialist or technocratic optimism (Beauvoir 1965: 91). This view of literature is exemplified in Beauvoir's novel, *Les Belles Images* (1966).

LES BELLES IMAGES (1966)

Beauvoir's fifth novel is a damning critique of mid 1960s' consumerist, technocratic society, set among affluent middle-class Parisians. Its main protagonist, Laurence, works in advertising, which enables Beauvoir, drawing upon her earlier work on myth, to expose the bourgeois patriarchal codes at work in popular culture of the 1960s. Like Beauvoir's final collection of short stories, *The Woman Destroyed* (1968), *Les Belles Images* is also feminist in that it contests patriarchal dominance and is marked by an awareness of how woman is constructed in patriarchal society, especially through language and representation (Heath 1989: 124–126).

STRUCTURALISM

Structuralism began in France in the 1950s and was initially associated with the anthropologist, Claude Lévi-Strauss and the literary critic, Roland Barthes. It has its roots in the work of the Swiss linguist, Ferdinand de Saussure (1857–1913), who pioneered the study of linguistic signs or semiology. He argued that the sign was composed of a signifier ('sound-image') and what is signified ('concept'), but the relationship between a word and what it designates is arbitrary. Signs only make meanings for us because they are part of a system of signs, each of which is relationally different. For example, we agree that the signifier 'dog' refers to the concept of a small mammal with four legs which makes the sound 'woof', but the choice of the signifier 'dog' is arbitrary, and relationally different to the signifier 'cat' and so on. So no word can be defined in isolation as it only assumes meaning in its relational difference to other words in the system. Language, for Saussure, meaningfully constitutes our world; it does not just label it. Saussure's ideas about language were adapted to analyse a range of signifying systems and their ideological functions, such as anthropology, psychoanalysis and modern culture, by figures such as Lévi-Strauss, Barthes, Lacan and Foucault. Structuralist analyses led to the rethinking of the idea of the human subject as transcendental and knowing, prevalent since the late eighteenth century, and the subject became characterised as an 'effect' (rather than a producer) of discourse.

Beauvoir views language as a powerful tool of social integration, for in exchanging language we reintegrate ourselves into the human community. She argues here that each individual is composed of all other individuals and can only understand him- or herself through intersubjective communication and understanding. This reflects her notion, explored in Chapters 1 and 2, that the Other is always already part of one's situation. The task of literature in this context is to render the singularity of individual experience as transparent as possible to other human beings, to safeguard the human dimension of experience from alienation by bureaucracy and technocracy (Beauvoir 1965: 92). Beauvoir defends committed literature here against what she perceives as the reactionary potential of the 'new novel'; yet, as noted above, she also defends a notion of situated subjectivity, developed in *Pyrrhus et Cinéas*, *The Ethics of Ambiguity* and *The Second Sex*, against the antihumanism of structuralism and an increasingly technocratic society of the 1960s (Kruks 1992: 91–92).

Beauvoir made several other important statements about literature in the 1960s and the 1970s which we will look at here. Two of these – 'My experience as a writer' ('Mon expérience d'écrivain') and 'Woman and creativity' ('La Femme et la création') were given as lectures during a visit to Japan which Beauvoir and Sartre made in 1966.

FICTION AND AUTOBIOGRAPHY

In 'My experience as a writer', Beauvoir argues that all writers express the lived meaning of being in the world in the literary work as a 'singular universal' (Beauvoir 1979a: 439). Taking the example of her first novel, *She Came to Stay*, she explains that she found a way of communicating a particular experience which was also a universal question, namely the problem of the Other. In this way, the creative work can lend a universal dimension to individual experience. Much of Beauvoir's discussion is taken up with an analysis of her use of different genres. She explains that she chooses to express herself in the essay form (as in *The Ethics of Ambiguity* and *The Second Sex*) when she has formulated her views on a subject. For Beauvoir, there are two forms of writing that express the lived meaning of 'being-in-the-world': fiction and autobiography.

Writing fiction allows Beauvoir to dispense with the pure facticity of the world (Beauvoir 1979a: 443). Our experience is 'detotalised' in that we cannot live all aspects at once and yet the novel can express the meanings which are at the horizon, but are not part of our experience. It can address the contradictions and ambiguities of experience. Beauvoir cites the example of *The Mandarins* (1954), in which two opposing views (through the focalisers of Henri and Anne) are represented. In this text, both Beauvoir's singular experience as an intellectual and the generality of the situation of left-wing intellectuals are represented. She rejects, however, the use of 'roman à clefs' (a novel which draws on real events and people) and 'roman à thèse' (a realistic and didactic novel which aims to promote a specific doctrine) for their falsification of the necessary creative work in novelwriting. However, one disadvantage of the novel form, in Beauvoir's view, is that it fails to represent the contingent and superfluous elements in lived experience, such as the meaningless trivia of everyday life before it assumes shape (if it ever does) as a significant event.

Autobiography, on the other hand, can incorporate the 'everyday', contingent elements of experience, although it must assume a universal dimension to engage readers. Referring to her own, massive autobiographical project upon which she embarked from the mid 1950s, Beauvoir explains that, when she uses the first-person pronoun in autobiography, she is sometimes referring to her own generation's experience of particular historical events, such as seeing the first Sputnik (earth-orbiting satellite) in 1957. In this way, her autobiographical project assumes a testimonial dimension, and for this reason, Beauvoir rejects the accusation of narcissism in writing several volumes of memoirs. The use of the autobiographical 'I' is also gendered, as she recognises that her autobiography also foregrounds a woman's perspective on historical events. In this way, developing her critique of history in *The Second Sex*, Beauvoir writes herself into the historical mainstream, thereby challenging the masculinism of a universalist perspective (Beauvoir 1979a: 450).

She also defends the literary craft of autobiographers, anticipating a criticism from the *Tel Quel* tendency that, drawing on Barthes's distinctions between 'authors' and 'writers', autobiography might be a merely factual document. Beauvoir argues that autobiography cannot be viewed as a factual document because, like fiction, it is rooted in lived experience. Writing autobiography requires a reconstruction of past events which are no longer readily accessible to the writer. In this context, she explains her choice of a chronological presentation of autobiographical events in the first three volumes of her memoirs as being motivated by her acute awareness of the temporal dimension of her

BARTHES, AUTHORS AND WRITERS

One of Barthes's most influential concepts is his distinction between 'authors' ('écrivains') and 'writers' (écrivants') (Barthes 1964: 185–193). He argues that the 'author' eschews language as a mimetic tool to represent the 'real' and explores the linguistic space; the 'writer', however, uses language instrumentally to communicate a particular, politicised vision of the world. In this context, Beauvoir's writing practice might be described as that of an 'écrivant'.

existence and of the importance of history. Temporality or the lived experience of time and the impact of historical events are, indeed, a key part of her 'situation' for Beauvoir. In *The Prime of Life*, for example, describing her initial response to the onset of the Second World War, she notes: 'History took hold of me and never let me go thereafter' (*PL*: 359) and it is this 'historicity' (or the state of being involved in the actual world as a concrete existent so as to possess a history) which is crucial in the autobiographical representation of her life.

A disadvantage of a chronological presentation of the life in auto-biography, however, is that it can appear to the reader to lack synthesis (Beauvoir 1979a: 453). Hence, the writer can never capture both the meaning of lived experience and the reality of that experience in a single type of writing. So Beauvoir argues that the novel, consequently, is necessary to represent the necessary meaning of lived experience, whereas autobiography can represent the facticity and contingency of that experience.

Beauvoir ends her discussion of writing by focusing on the role of the reader. Like Sartre in *What is Literature?*, Beauvoir sees writing crucially as an appeal to the freedom of the reader. She argues that the literary work is the privileged locus of intersubjectivity and that the writer's task is to break through the separation between individual human beings, for they are linked, in fact, by what separates them. In writing about the most apparently personal experiences, a writer can attain general truths which are recognised by readers. The example of her account of her mother's illness and death from intestinal cancer related in *A Very Easy Death* (1964) is instructive here, for, although the precise circumstances of her mother's death are unique, nevertheless many readers identified with Beauvoir's experience of losing a parent to cancer. In this way, writing and reading act as cathartic activities both for writers and readers and enable them to share their most profound and painful experiences. In Beauvoir's view, this fundamental function of literature – to communicate and share human experience – was utterly neglected by writing associated with the *Tel Quel* tendency in France in the 1960s.

WOMAN AND CREATIVITY

In a second lecture on 'woman and creativity', Beauvoir develops her analyses on this subject in *The Second Sex* (*SS*: 713–723). In the 1966

'A ROOM OF ONE'S OWN' (1929)

In this classic feminist essay, Virginia Woolf (1882–1941) argues that women have struggled with formidable educational, financial and social obstacles which have prevented them from creating great works of literature (using the hypothetical example of Shakespeare's sister, whose aspirations end in suicide). She contends that women will not be able to write well and freely until they have the privacy, space and freedom implied by 'a room of one's own' and 'five hundred a year'. She acknowledges the achievements of women writers of the past and of women novelists, arguing that fiction-writing, as a more recent literary genre, was well suited to women. Increased equality would enable women to become poets, as well as novelists. In the final chapter, Woolf explores the relationship between androgyny and creativity.

lecture, she seeks to answer the question of why women have not achieved as much in creative terms as men. Citing Virginia Woolf's influential essay, 'A room of one's own' (1929), Beauvoir argues that the room in question is both a reality and a symbol, for woman needs to belong to herself and to have material freedom in order to write and to accomplish creatively.

But, traditionally, woman belongs to her husband and to her children. Talent is not enough, for women, like men, need favourable social conditions in which to develop their talent. Despite gaining the right to vote and an increasingly free choice of professional activity, Beauvoir argues that women still do not enjoy equality of opportunity with men. This is because there are statistically fewer women in major professions, which militates against their achievement. They also do not earn as much as men or carry out the same level of professional activities as men. Women, unlike men, are obliged to divide their energy and commitment between work and home, which impedes their ambitions. Moreover, argues Beauvoir in this survey of women's situation, women's success is often a threat to their partner or the likelihood of getting a partner. So women's professional underachievement can be explained by their overall situation.

In the context of women's creativity, women are not usually encouraged to become artists or writers. In the realm of visual arts in which careers are expensive to undertake, women have more limited access to money than male artists and they cannot count on the level of support and respect that men receive. Women encounter social hostility if they try to live a bohemian, artistic lifestyle. Beauvoir cites the example of her friend, the sculptor Alberto Giacometti (1901–1966), whose unconventional lifestyle and creative freedom would have been impossible for a woman.

Beauvoir argues that, in addition to external obstacles, women face psychological obstacles to their creativity which result from their alienated situation. Nevertheless, literature is a more accessible sphere to women because it costs less to pursue a literary career and most middle-class girls learn how to write. But women still do not achieve great success as writers (Beauvoir 1979b: 466). Why? Beauvoir argues that women still do not approach writing as a vocation, but more as a hobby, because they are not encouraged in their literary ambitions. It is instructive here to note that Beauvoir herself was encouraged in her childhood writing and reading and that she initially took her own inspiration from the British woman writer, George Eliot (1819–1880) (*MDD*: 140–141). While boys seek to exceed the achievements of their fathers, girls have poor maternal role models if their mothers have accepted a traditional role as wife and mother. Girls are encouraged to believe that their families or their future husbands will take responsibility for them. Consequently they do not experience the same degree of existential anguish and abandonment and do not feel compelled to create a work which throws the world into question (Beauvoir 1979b: 469–470). Women are not brought up to take responsibility for the world and so are less likely to fundamentally question the world and how it works in their creative activity. Women also lack the extremism and patience of genius which can lead to great achievement (Beauvoir 1979b: 472–473). But all these factors must be viewed in the light of creativity being a construct, not a natural activity. Creativity is socially conditioned and, as long as women do not benefit from the same opportunities and patronage as men, the results of their creativity will necessarily be less impressive. Beauvoir is not saying that women cannot achieve artistic and literary greatness, but rather that the conditions (in the 1960s) for their full achievement did not yet exist.

Beauvoir's views on creativity have been challenged, for example by Christine Battersby, who argues that she operates with a Romantic notion of genius and creativity in *The Second Sex* and in her lecture on woman and creativity (Battersby 1989: 150–154):

> De Beauvoir still measures all cultural achievements against the paradigm personality of Romantic genius who walks that narrow path between sanity and madness [. . .] De Beauvoir does not recognise that the Romantic genius must also be *like* a woman – but not a woman. Instead, she internalises the Romantic version of man's past: that defines genius in terms of the *male* psyche, and then concludes that in the whole of Western culture there has never been one (real) female genius.
>
> (Battersby 1989: 152)

In an assessment of Battersby's argument, it is important to remember that Beauvoir is not claiming that women cannot be original or be geniuses, but rather that gendered roles and spheres of activity restrict most women from achieving highly original work. Nevertheless, as Battersby notes, Beauvoir's examples of male genius, which include Van Gogh, 'nourished' by frequenting prostitutes, may have the effect of glamorising a particular form of genius – the solitary Bohemian male – and using it as the model for creative originality.

The final text we will look at here which will enable us to assess Beauvoir's views on women's relationship to language and literature is an interview she gave in 1977 to a US academic, Alice Jardine. Like her statements in the 1960s on literature, *Tel Quel* and the 'new novel', Beauvoir again responds to current developments in 'women's writing' in the 1970s, particularly to the question of 'écriture féminine'.

As noted in Chapter 4, Beauvoir became active in the French women's liberation movement (Mouvement de libération de la femme, or MLF) in the early 1970s, and worked with materialist feminists, influenced by Marxism, on a range of issues such as abortion and battered women. The 1970s also represented a boom for women writers, many of whom were marked by second-wave feminism and who sought to articulate their experience in patriarchal society in diverse ways (Fallaize 1993: 16–17). Among French women's writing in the 1970s, one can identify two broad tendencies: 'écriture féminine', rooted in psychoanalysis, and a new realism, rooted in historical materialism, exemplified by writers such as Annie Ernaux (1940–) and Claire Etcherelli (1934–). Beauvoir rejected 'écriture féminine', as we shall see, and was intellectually closer to the materialist feminist writers and theorists.

In the 1977 interview to be considered here, Beauvoir explains her rejection of 'écriture féminine'. She says that it is esoteric, in her view,

HELENE CIXOUS AND 'ECRITURE FEMININE'

Hélène Cixous is a key differentialist French feminist writer and thinker who has been concerned with writing, subjectivity and sexuality. She emerged in France during the post-1968 period of second-wave feminism and was associated with the *des femmes* publishing house, set up by 'Psychanalyse et politique', a faction within the French feminist movement. Cixous is interested in sexual difference and seeks to envisage female subjectivity outside the constraints of phallogocentrism. This term, 'phallogocentrism', derived from Jacques Derrida, is coined from 'phallocentrism' (or privileging the phallus as dominant signifier) and 'logocentrism' (or privileging the word as a means to full truth and presence). Phallogocentrism refers to the dominance of patriarchy through language and representation and has been expressed by the Marxist literary theorist, Terry Eagleton, as 'cocksureness', or the mechanism by which 'those who wield sexual and social power maintain their grip' (Eagleton 1983: 189). Differentialist feminists, such as Cixous, used the work of Freud, Lacan and Derrida, especially, to recover this repressed feminine difference within patriarchal culture and thought. In *The Newly Born Woman* (1975), Cixous provides a critique of patriarchal binaries which govern Western thought, in which the second term of the binary has traditionally been associated with the feminine and devalued as such – for example, 'active/passive', 'logos/pathos', 'civilisation/nature'. Cixous developed a writing project to deconstruct these binary oppositions, i.e. 'écriture féminine' (translated as 'feminine writing' or 'writing the body'). 'Ecriture féminine' is experimental writing, practised by women or men, which is marked by 'jouissance' (pleasure or excess). It inscribes feminine difference, formerly repressed in the masculine symbolic order, and privileges the pre-Oedipal mother–child relation over the Symbolic. 'Ecriture féminine' texts are characterised by the use of gaps, ambiguities, disruption, shifting genre and register, using the myriad possibilities of language, stripped of its patriarchal project. The writing practice of Cixous, Colette, Virginia Woolf, James Joyce and Jean Genet are possible examples of 'écriture féminine'.

and erroneous to seek out a woman's language (Beauvoir 1979d: 230). She does not accept that there might be a 'women's language' and says that 'women simply have to steal the instrument [. . .] steal it and use it for their own good'. She says that men as well as women write with their body when they write because 'everything is implicated in the work of a writer'. Asked about the role of the unconscious in writing, Beauvoir argues that it is not possible to tap deliberately into the unconscious in the writing process, although a writer cannot stop unconscious effects from being manifested in her or his writing. She argues that 'we must use language. If it is used in a feminist perspective, with a feminist sensibility, language will find itself changed in a feminist manner' (Beauvoir 1979d: 230) As we have already noted, Beauvoir sees writing as the product of the writer's entire situation.

She does recognise, however, that women will write in different ways to male writers when they write about their experience as women, but says that there are topics which are common to both women and men. In her view, 'woman is at the same time universal and a woman, just as a man is universal and a male' (Beauvoir 1979d: 231). Beauvoir warns against putting women writers into a ghetto and says: 'I want them to be singular and universal at the same time'. This accords with her earlier statements in 'Mon expérience d'écrivain', in which she argues that literature should deal with the most singular experiences to communicate the universal dimensions of the human condition. In the case of her own writings, Beauvoir says that they could not have been written by a man because her work is marked by a feminine sensibility and her feminine situation in the world (Beauvoir 1979d: 233). She contends that, although male writers, such as Stendhal, can portray women characters extremely well from the outside, only women can represent the lived experience of women – a task which she expressly undertakes in her fiction of the 1960s and, more generally, in her own volumes of memoirs. In this context, writing autobiography can be an important catharsis for women at the moment of their emancipation (Beauvoir 1979d: 234).

In this brief survey of Beauvoir's thinking on literature, we see that certain of her philosophical concepts, such as 'situation', 'alienation' and 'woman as absolute Other', are deeply imbricated in her notions about writing, language and their relationship to gender. Rejecting what she saw as the elitism and idealism of developments in the 1970s, such as 'écriture féminine', Beauvoir consistently argued that writing had to be rooted in the material realities of all human lives. Her existential humanist perspective sees writing as an ethical appeal to the Other as reader — an opportunity to communicate the particularity of individual situations to each other and thereby surmount the anguish of the human condition. Yet her own textual practice of fiction-writing from the late 1930s to the late 1960s is increasingly marked by her awareness of women's alienated situation in patriarchal society. In this way, Beauvoir's practice of committed writing had developed by the 1960s into an acute ethical critique of patriarchal society.

SUMMARY

Beauvoir argues that the metaphysical novel functioning as a bridge between literature and philosophy can represent the concrete singularity of human experience in its historical and eternal dimensions. Her notion of literature as necessarily 'committed' has formal implications for her textual practice; for example, she represents the ambiguity and contradictions of existence as experienced by situated characters. In Beauvoir's view, authentic literature transcends the separation and alienation between human beings if it constitutes a genuine quest and communicative encounter between author and reader. She rejected what she viewed as the elitist notion of a specifically feminine language and writing, arguing that women must appropriate language and writing for their own purposes, which may coincide with those of male writers. In her later fictional writing, she attempts to represent the feminine as a site of resistance to patriarchal ideology. Beauvoir recognised that women's lived experience of their situation will mark their textual practice.

6

AGE

In 1970, Beauvoir published the second major study of her career, *Old Age*. In this chapter, we will look at the key ideas of this text and how Beauvoir develops certain of her arguments from *The Second Sex* in the context of ageing.

Why was she interested in ageing? In the final volume of her memoirs, *All Said and Done* (1972), Beauvoir explains that she decided to study old age following the outcry from her readers over her discussion of her own ageing at the end of *Force of Circumstance*, the third volume of her memoirs (*ASD*: 146). She recognised that the process of ageing and the treatment of the aged in society were taboo subjects. Seeing in *Old Age* 'the counterpart of *The Second Sex*', Beauvoir was attracted by the demystifying potential of her study. Just as she had attempted in *The Second Sex* to dismantle the naturalising, oppressive discourses of femininity which maintained women in a state of subordination, in *Old Age* she set out to expose the situation of old people. Nevertheless, as we will see, there are certain organisational and focal differences between the two texts.

At a personal level, *Old Age*, like *The Second Sex*, is also driven by Beauvoir's personal quest for knowledge: 'I was on the threshold of old age, and I wished to know the bounds and the nature of the aged state' (*ASD*: 147). *Old Age*, then, similarly provides a critique of universalism. It is informed by her belief in the philosophical relevance of singular individual human experience as it intersects with the collective human situation.

Prior to her work on *Old Age*, Beauvoir confronted a singular example of ageing, illness and death when her mother became ill and died of intestinal cancer in 1963. She related this experience in *A Very Easy Death* (1964), a bedside biographical testimony which constitutes a case study of certain of the generalised arguments in *Old Age* (Tidd 1999: 165). As in *Old Age*, Beauvoir is concerned in this text with the lived experience of the ill, ageing body and the ethical issues surrounding the ending of life. As she would later argue in *Old Age*, although death is represented here as a democratic event, the conditions in which each human subject experiences death are highly variable, depending on familial and economic circumstances, among other factors. In the case of Beauvoir's mother, she is able to end her days in an expensive Paris clinic, although her daughter is acutely aware that this is a privileged experience of ageing, illness and death. Beauvoir would subsequently expose the diversity of the experience of ageing from a theoretical perspective in *Old Age*.

The book is divided into two parts: Part I is devoted to 'Old age seen from without' or from biological, ethnological, historical and contemporary perspectives. Here, Beauvoir focuses on ageing as the object of knowledge, appraised from an external perspective. Part II is entitled 'The being-in-the-world' and deals with the lived experiences of old people from their own point of view.

In the Introduction, society's attitudes to ageing and old age are revealed as deeply ambivalent. Old age is also ill-defined, varying 'according to era and place'; unlike adulthood, it is not marked by any initiation ceremony (*OA*: 9). Unlike children and teenagers, old people are not regarded as a specific consumer market; they are classified as economically non-active and as burdensome to the active population. Bourgeois ideology aims to separate workers and old people, so that the latter are viewed as different, alien beings, required to be passive, virtuous and serenely disengaged from the world. Old people are therefore an alienated group and this alienation begins at the level of individual subjectivity in a person's refusal to recognise themselves as a future old person. Beauvoir argues that it is impossible to provide a universal definition of old age because it is experienced differently according to the state of individual health, financial and family circumstances, which are partly governed by the class struggle which divides old people as a group into the privileged and the exploited. As in *The Second Sex*, she explains that 'old age can only be understood as a whole: it is not solely a biological, but also a *cultural* fact' (*OA*: 20). But, crucially, it is important to remember that Beauvoir does not consider old age as a universal category: it only appears that way because the diversity of experiences of ageing are concealed by ageist images and myths promoted by capitalist and patriarchal discourses. For example, women over seventy years old are often stereotypically portrayed in the media (if they are portrayed at all) as non-sexual beings or as out of touch with contemporary life or as a passive burden on their relatives, even though that may only correlate to a minority of older women's experiences.

Initially, Beauvoir describes the physical and physiological aspects of ageing, noting that 'old age in its pure state' is rare because of the relationship between old age and disease (*OA*: 34). Old age is the most favourable time for psychosomatic disorders; disease in the elderly is closely related to psychological factors. This is not because old people are intrinsic imaginary invalids, but because they are encouraged by an ageist society to live inauthentically, as women are encouraged to live inauthentically in patriarchal society, as we saw in *The Second Sex*. So, hypochondria in the old is a reaction to their overall situation in an ageist society.

There are, however, great biological differences between individuals of the same age. To understand the meaning and reality of old age, argues Beauvoir, it is necessary to examine how old people have been treated and represented at different times and at different places, for historical and geographical determinants are also decisive in shaping individual experiences of old age. Analysing old age from an ethnological perspective, Beauvoir does not identify a single element in the social organisation of tribal societies which determines the treatment of old people. It is, however, evident that 'an old person has a greater chance of survival in wealthy societies than in poor, and among settled rather than nomadic people' (*OA*: 90).

In addition to these factors, old age has neither the same meaning nor the same consequences for men as for women (*OA*: 95). Indeed, following her analyses in *The Second Sex*, we would expect Beauvoir to recognise gender as another determinant in the experience of old age. For post-menopausal women, they are no longer regarded as 'a being with a sex'. In matrilinear societies (in which social organisation and descent is organised through the female line), however, older women will play an important cultural, religious and political role. Nevertheless, they generally experience an inferior social status to men. Explicitly linking her analyses of gender in *The Second Sex*, Beauvoir notes:

> Among primitive peoples, the aged man is truly the Other [. . .] In masculine myths, the woman, the Other, appears as an idol and as a sex-object at one and the same time. Similarly, for other reasons and in another manner, the old man in those societies is both a sub-man and a superman. He is decrepit and useless: but he is also the intercessor, the magician, the priest – below or beyond the human state, and often both together.
>
> (*OA*: 97)

Concluding her survey of primitive tribal attitudes to the old, Beauvoir notes: 'the status of the old man is never won but always granted'.

In her subsequent survey of 'Old age in historical societies' in the third chapter, Beauvoir draws on both historical and literary sources, as in *The Second Sex*. She argues that old people have never played a consistently determining role in history, although certain well-organised societies have drawn upon the experience of its elder members. She highlights that historical records of patriarchal societies ignore the fate of older women, because the power struggles which shape history occur between men. As in *The Second Sex*, women are positioned as the absolute Other. Again, throughout history, favourable economic circumstances are decisive in improving old people's situation and longevity. For this reason, accounts of old age are exclusively authored by a privileged elderly elite, a fact which dictates the type of source material examined in the second part of *Old Age* (*OA*: 240). When the ruling class has comprised or been influenced by old men, value has been attributed to great age. From the nineteenth century onwards, there were increased numbers of poor among the elderly and the ruling class was no longer able to ignore them, so they were undervalued. Class struggle was more decisive than any inter-generational conflict in how old people were treated (*OA*: 242).

In Chapter 4, Beauvoir argues that the elderly are treated scandalously in Western contemporary society. Drawing on Sartre's discussion of reciprocity and praxis (or uniting political theory and practice in order to change both oneself and society) in *Critique of*

Dialectical Reason (1960), Beauvoir argues (as she had argued in *The Ethics of Ambiguity*) that reciprocity demands a mutual recognition of each other's transcendence. But, in the case of an old person, 'he is defined by an exis, not by a praxis: a being, not a doing' (*OA*: 244). The old person is defined by their unavoidable relationship to death, which is not part of any personal project; for this reason, active members of the community do not recognise themselves in the old person, regarding him or her as a member of a different species. Although there are certain similarities between the situation of the child and the old person, society projects its future on to the child, whereas the old person is 'no more than a corpse under suspended sentence'. Adults treat old people with a characteristic duplicity: by demonstrating a degree of respect which is simultaneously marked by a vested interest to treat the old person as inferior and to convince them of their decline.

As in *The Second Sex*, Beauvoir demonstrates an acute awareness in *Old Age* of power relations between the ruling group (economically active men) and the oppressed (old people). The power struggle between the generations also has a moral aspect in that society requires that the elderly should conform to a certain image and role, which governs their appearance, sexuality and activities. In this, the situations of old people and women are similar, for both are required to conform to conventions laid down by economically active members of the patriarchy. In this respect, *Old Age*, like *Pyrrhus et Cinéas*, *The Ethics of Ambiguity* and *The Second Sex*, is both descriptive and normative (Lundgren-Gothlin 1996: 152). In other words, Beauvoir's discussion of ageing has an implicit ethical purpose in mind: to expose the scandalous treatment of old people with a view to improving it (Miller 2001: 136).

Beauvoir then demonstrates how material provision for elderly people is generally inadequate in most Western capitalist countries, except in Denmark, Norway and Sweden. As we have already noted, this is because old people are defined as passive beings rather than as active contributors to society. Society's preoccupation with the economically active members of the population entails that retired people are removed from the labour market early, regardless of their capacity to continue working, and are made to constitute a burden on the active population. Consequently, old people, especially men and manual workers, find it difficult to make the transition from work to retirement (*OA*: 300). One unfortunate aspect of the situation of old people is their powerlessness to change it. As Beauvoir argues in the case of women's situation in *The Second Sex*, old people do not constitute a socially cohesive group and consequently cannot exercise any bargaining power that such group cohesion might bring (*OA*: 310). This lack of social cohesion among the elderly is less in evidence these days, of course, with the advent of older political activists in the 'grey lobby', who regularly campaign for better pension rights, among other issues.

LIVED EXPERIENCE

In the second part of her study, Beauvoir concentrates on the lived experience of old age – from the subject's point of view. This second part is divided into four chapters, dealing respectively with the bodily experience of old age; the old person's experience of time, activity and history; old age and everyday life; and some examples of old age as experienced by well-known cultural figures. The focus on the diverse lived experience of old people is consonant with her phenomenological method, which focuses on old people as situated human beings (Miller 2001: 131). This allows Beauvoir to dispense with the ageist and sexist stereotypes, myths and images surrounding old people (Miller 2001: 135).

In Chapter 5, old age is represented for the outsider as a dialectical relationship between the person's being as he or she defines it objectively and the self-awareness that the person acquires by means of that outsider. For the old person, it is 'the Other' (the person he or she is for the outsider) who is old and that Other is the old person. As Miller notes, 'the phenomenological lived experience of the elderly is one in which they are both subject and object' (Miller 2001: 144). Ageing leaves an indisputable mark on our being, corresponding to biological phenomena which may be detected by medical examination (*OA*: 316). Old age cannot be experienced inwardly as we appear outwardly to other people. Ultimately, the ageing subject has to accept the Other's view of him or her as an old person (*OA*: 323). We can become old before our time or try to stay young until we die – either way, our attitude towards ageing will express our relationship with the world in general. But the physical aspects of ageing cannot be avoided and Beauvoir rejects claims by moralists and spiritualists that physical decline brings compensations (*OA*: 351–352).

In the case of old people's sexuality, a range of responses to the reality of ageing is possible. Although, at a biological level, women's sexuality is less affected by age than men's, older heterosexual women have a less active sex life than their male counterparts. Older women are less attractive to younger men than older men are to younger women. This, Beauvoir explains, is because 'socially men, whatever their age, are subjects, and women are objects, relative beings' (*OA*: 387). As in *The Second Sex*, the situation of lesbians casts useful light on the overall situation of women, for lesbians are sexually active well into their eighties, demonstrating that women's sexual drive continues well into old age.

Beauvoir argues that ageing transforms our relationship to time:

> for human reality, existing means existing in time: in the present we look towards the future by means of plans that go beyond our past, in which our activities fall lifeless, frozen and loaded with passive demands. Age changes our relationship with time: as the years go by our future shortens, while our past grows heavier.

> (*OA*: 402)

The old person experiences memory as increasingly unreliable and fragmentary in advancing age, and the past is not usefully available. The future seems closed, so time appears to pass more quickly. In an existentialist context, the temporal reality of old people means that they exist in a perpetual present, for they are cut off from the past and they are unable to project themselves into the future in authentic activity, grounded by a project. Yet most old people refuse time and embrace their past, setting up a fixed essence of themselves to ward off the decline of age (*OA*: 403). Beauvoir identifies three forms of memory: sensor-motor memory, based on habit and automatic forms of behaviour; autistic memory, governed by the dynamics of the unconscious, in which the subject relives past impressions in the present; and social memory, which reconstructs past facts. Only social memory allows us to construct our own autobiographical narrative under certain conditions. Yet, the 'for-itself', in adulthood, is perpetually prey to the ontological disappointment of being unable to possess his or her life. In the case of the old person, she or he is more heavily burdened by what Sartre terms 'the practico-inert', for any project that would ground his or her being is frozen. Old people identify themselves with

'THE PRACTICO-INERT'

This term used in Sartre's *Critique of Dialectical Reason*, means the reified form of all an individual's past actions in their relationships to other people and things. Praxis assumes an inertia of its own so that it can 'respond' by generating a counter-praxis. In *Old Age*, Beauvoir gives the example of the whole formed by the books she has written (constituting 'praxis'), which exist outside her as her works and define her as their author (*OA*: 415). If the fact of their existence and her authorship entailed any unenvisaged consequence in the initial project of writing those books (such as her arrest or persecution), it would constitute an example of 'counter-praxis'.

the times in which they carried out their projects and, consequently, become survivors from a past age. Most people's idea of death is that it is 'unrealisable'. This is because the 'for-itself' or transcendent human subject cannot reach death nor project itself towards it: it is the external limit of a person's possibilities and not a possibility that they choose. A person is dead for other people, not for themselves (*OA*: 491). Knowledge of mortality is therefore abstract and assumed from the Other's view.

The absence of major projects in old people's lives is a further factor that contributes to their lack of interest in life and destroys their desire for knowledge. Using their old age as an excuse for any failings only further alienates them from other people and confirms their socially inferior status (*OA*: 514). Old people then adopt an attitude of defensiveness and experience self-disgust and occasional depression (*OA*: 523). Few old people have the opportunity of seizing the liberatory advantages of old age, such as being freed from the obligations of social and professional roles. Although old age might ideally be a time when people could 'let their hair down', in reality, their social and material marginalisation often renders them more dependent on friends and family than earlier in their lives. With this dependence comes loss of autonomy and a need to conform to others' views. This said, Beauvoir notes that heterosexual women rather than men are likely to experience old age as liberating: 'it is for women in particular that the last age is a liberation: all their lives they were subjected to their husbands and given over to the care of their children; now at last they can look after themselves' (*OA*: 543).

In the final chapter, Beauvoir describes how people's earlier choices can condition the experience of their old age by citing seven cases of old age exemplified by well-known cultural figures, namely the nineteenth-century writer, Victor Hugo (1802–1885); the sixteenth-century artist, Michelangelo Buonarroti (1475–1564); the nineteenth-century composer, Giuseppe Verdi (1813–1901); the psychoanalysts, Lou-Andréas Salomé (1861–1937) and Sigmund Freud (1856–1939); the writer and historian, François-René Chateaubriand (1768–1848); and the Romantic poet, Alphonse de Lamartine (1790–1869). But in all of these cases, there is, argues Beauvoir, no reason to suppose that a successful earlier life will result in a comfortable and productive old age. For example, in the case of Freud, despite his lengthy and successful career in psychoanalysis and the professional eminence which he achieved, his old age was a trial to him because of his poor health (he underwent twenty-three operations in the last sixteen years of his life), the rise of Nazism which entailed him having to leave Austria, where he had lived all his life, to escape anti-Semitic persecution, and his fears over the future of the discipline of psychoanalysis to which he had dedicated his life.

Beauvoir concludes that 'old age is life's parody, whereas death transforms life into destiny' (*OA*: 599). To avoid this, individuals should pursue ends that give their existence meaning, although this is only possible for a privileged sector of society. The alienation that most people experience during their working lives prepares a bleak and poverty-stricken old age. Indicting the human wastage incurred by capitalism, Beauvoir argues that 'society cares about the individual only in so far as he is profitable'. This is a moral indictment of society – 'old age exposes the failure of our entire civilization' – and she advocates a radical transformation of the conditions of life to remedy the alienation experienced by young and old alike (*OA*: 603–604).

Approaching the subject of old age partly from a Marxist perspective, Beauvoir identifies that the wastage and alienation of old people in society is mainly the result of capitalism's emphasis on the economically active sector of the population. However, the anguish and rejection of the experience of ageing are also related to aspects of the subject's situation, such as his or her experience of ontological abandonment, embodiment, possibilities of freedom and reciprocal relationships with others, and attitude to death – issues which Beauvoir addresses in *Pyrrhus et Cinéas*, *The Ethics of Ambiguity* and *The Second Sex*, as we saw in Chapters 2 and 3.

Beauvoir's approach to the study of ageing is impressively wide-ranging, drawing on biology, sociology, history, psychology and anthropology to understand the diversity of the lived experience of ageing. She does not offer the reader any detailed blueprint for transforming the situation of old people in society; the importance of *Old Age* lies in its demystifying and descriptive force. When it was published in 1970, it constituted a devastating exposé of the plight of old people by a major cultural figure on the international post-war stage. It appeared just after the publication of a major report into the social problems of the aged in France, so Beauvoir's study aroused much interest (*ASD*: 148). Unusually in her career, her study was praised by both left- and right-wing critical opinion. It was also applauded by gerontologists who praised Beauvoir for breaking the conspiracy of silence surrounding old age (*ASD*: 150).

Often viewed as a counterpart to *The Second Sex*, there are nevertheless some differences of approach and focus. For example, the discussion of biology is sketchier in *Old Age* than in *The Second Sex* – perhaps because biologism was a powerful first line of defence for antifeminists, it required a more detailed treatment. Her treatment of myths and images in *Old Age* also takes into account the diversity of experiences that the category 'old age' encompasses in ways that the analysis of myths and images of femininity in *The Second Sex* does not (Bergoffen 1997: 187). In the second part of her examination of old people's experiences of being old, there is a narrower range of sources than in *The Second Sex*. Beauvoir acknowledges that, in *Old Age*, she was obliged to draw mainly on privileged old people's accounts of being old. It lacks the 'concealed, first-hand ethnography' of *The Second Sex* (Okely 1986: 124). It also draws heavily on accounts of ageing by writers and cultural figures, which, for some readers, may diminish its documentary value (Keefe 1983: 137). However, as we saw in Chapter 5, Beauvoir justifies the inclusion of literary sources in her philosophical and socio-political writing on the grounds that, like Hegel and Kierkegaard in their philosophical writing, it enables her to emphasise the role and value of subjective experience. In the case of *Old Age*, accounts of subjective experience are particularly important because one of Beauvoir's main arguments is that there is no universal experience of old age, but a collection of diverse experiences which are dependent on the interaction of physiological, psychological, familial, economic, historical, socio-cultural and geographical variables.

As in *The Second Sex*, Beauvoir makes use of key concepts from existential phenomenology developed in the 1940s, such as situation, anguish, reciprocity, project and inauthenticity. She also draws on concepts from Sartre's more recent work, such as 'the practico-inert' and the relationship between reciprocity and praxis from the *Critique of Dialectical Reason*.

Despite recognising that a radical transformation of society is necessary to improve the situation of old people, she no longer expresses any faith in socialism as a revolutionary force acting on society, unlike the conclusion to her 1949 study of gender. In *Old Age*, the plight of old people in socialist countries is demonstrated to be only marginally better than in capitalist ones (*OA*: 617–634).

Beauvoir also demonstrates how ageism and sexism are often combined. As Marks suggests, ageist discourses appear to be imbricated historically with the elaboration of misogynist discourses on female embodiment: 'the disgust and fear provoked by the female body in Western discourses are related to similar effects provoked by old bodies' (Marks 1986: 194). The subject's reluctance to embrace ageing is, in part, a refusal to accept the image of their changed embodiment in the look of the Other. As noted above, the subject's internalisation and acceptance of old age is a dialectical process, a mediated relationship between the subject's being as he or she defines it objectively and the self-awareness that the subject acquires by means of the Other. Consequently, the experience of ageing is a troubling ambiguity, characterised by 'doubling', in which the old person experiences him- or herself as both subject and object (Miller 2001: 147).

In an interview in 1978, Beauvoir elaborated on a number of issues in *Old Age* (Beauvoir 1984: 84–93). Here, she describes her own experience of old age as an 'unrealisable' in so far as it is 'a state that obtains for other people, but not so much for oneself'. She also identifies the worst aspect of ageing as the closure of the future in an old person's life, describing it as 'a step out of the infinite into the finite' (Beauvoir 1984: 88). She rejects the notion that old age is more difficult for women than for men because men generally have more access to power and responsibility than women in their working lives and, consequently, have more to lose on retirement. Moreover, stripped of their power, ageing men have less power over their partners and so women often gain power and responsibility in retirement. Women also usually have their domestic role in retirement, especially if they have not worked outside the home, and consequently survive retirement and old age better than men (Beauvoir 1984: 92).

Old Age is the final theoretical text in which, building on her earlier work in *Pyrrhus et Cinéas*, *The Ethics of Ambiguity* and *The Second Sex*, Beauvoir seeks to analyse the diverse situations of old people, positioned as society's 'Others'. Drawing on an impressive range of disciplines, and adopting both a Marxist and existentialist-phenomenological approach to her topic, Beauvoir exposes the troubling ambiguity of old age.

SUMMARY

In *Old Age*, Beauvoir argues that there is no universal experience of ageing; it depends on the interaction of a range of physiological, psychological, familial, historical, geographical and socio-cultural variables. Like her analysis of gender in *The Second Sex*, old age is represented as a *cultural* not a natural fact. Her study is both descriptive and normative in that she adopts an ethical viewpoint towards her topic. She aims to dismantle the myths and images perpetuated by bourgeois ideology to conceal the diverse realities of ageing. Women, for example, experience ageing differently to men because of their different situation in patriarchal society. For the old person, it is 'the Other' (the person he or she is for the outsider) who is old, not the person they experience themselves to be. Old age is consequently an 'unrealisable' in which the old person experiences themselves as subject but are perceived as an object by outsiders. The experience of ageing involves a dialectical relationship with other people in which ultimately the old person is obliged to accept the external image of themselves. Like women in *The Second Sex*, the old person is 'Other' to the economically active members of society. The old person is alienated, defined by an exis, not a praxis. They are deprived of authentic projects which would allow them to transcend the given. Old people are also divided from each other by the class struggle which governs the diverse experiences of ageing. Only a complete social transformation would transform the scandalous treatment of old people in Western, capitalist societies.

AFTER BEAUVOIR

Simone de Beauvoir's thought has been profoundly influential across a broad range of disciplines and continues to be explored and debated around the world. During the 1980s and 1990s, following Beauvoir's death in 1986 and the fiftieth anniversary of the publication of *The Second Sex* in 1999, there has been renewed and vigorous interest in her work. This is the result of (1) careful rereadings of Beauvoir's texts which recognise the originality and continuing relevance of her thought, and (2) the generalised impact of feminist approaches to philosophy, literary theory, history, theology and the sciences. It is beyond the scope of this concluding section to account for all the theorists and writers across the disciplines who are indebted to her work. Instead, we will look at the legacy of her philosophical thought and some of the recent ways in which it has been critiqued and developed. Even so, such an overview will not be exhaustive as Beauvoir's writings are subject to a wealth of rereadings on a continuing basis. Consulting works cited in the 'Further Reading' section of this volume will enable you to develop further your knowledge of aspects of her work and its legacy.

BEAUVOIR'S IMPACT ON SECOND-WAVE FEMINIST THOUGHT

The science historian Donna Haraway has argued that 'despite important differences, all the modern feminist meanings of gender have roots in Simone de Beauvoir's claim that "one is not born a woman"' (Haraway 1991: 131). Indeed, the notion of gender as a construct, rather than a natural, undisputed 'fact' of identity, is so deeply embedded in much second-wave feminist thinking that it has become part of feminism's conceptual framework. Beauvoir's notion of woman as being positioned as relative absolute 'Other' to man as the masculine universal subject is also fundamental to twentieth-century feminist theory.

In the third millennium, *The Second Sex* is considered a foundational text for modern feminism and, even though subsequent well-known theorists such as Luce Irigaray and Julia Kristeva are critical of Beauvoir's arguments, much of second-wave feminism, in both the Anglo-American and the French contexts, would be unthinkable without her work. Moreover, it continues to engage major feminist theorists, such as the French philosopher, Michèle Le Doeuff, the gender theorist, Judith Butler, and the feminist theorist and literary critic, Toril Moi.

In France, the legacy of Beauvoir's thought is extremely difficult to measure and is evolving as new generations of feminist thinkers engage with her work and as cross-disciplinary feminist methodologies develop in the French academy. Some consider that Beauvoir supplied the theoretical apparatus to the post-1968 French women's movement and argue that *The Second Sex* is its most important theoretical work (Rodgers 1998: 23). In this context, the psychoanalytic writer, Elisabeth Roudinesco, credits Beauvoir with being the first thinker in France to link explicitly the question of sexuality with political emancipation (Roudinesco 1986: 511–512). Others, such as the philosopher and historian, Geneviève Fraisse, recognise that Beauvoir put the question of sexual difference on the philosophical map in her formulation of woman as 'Other'(Rodgers 1998: 24).

In Chapters 3 and 4, it was argued that, in the 1970s and 1980s in France, Beauvoir's thought was closer to materialist feminisms (associated for example with Monique Wittig and Christine Delphy, to be considered in more detail below) and, outside France, inspired Anglo-American feminist thinkers such as Friedan, Millett, Greer and

Firestone. As we saw in Chapter 4, French radical materialist feminism contends that gender inequalities are rooted in social practices, rather than in ideas or in individual psyches. Radical materialist feminism sees psychological differences between men and women as *caused* by social inequality, rather than psychosexual difference *resulting* in social inequality. In common with Beauvoir's thinking on gender, French radical materialist feminism is anti-biologistic and anti-essentialist in that it is opposed to any notion of an essential gender identity. It does not accept that gender is a 'natural' phenomenon, but argues instead that it is a social product. So it is opposed to the idea that women's difference can be a starting point for their liberation, because this 'difference' is already socially constructed and only defines women in relation to men. As Delphy has argued, moreover, hierarchy is imbricated in the notion of all differences, not just sexual difference (Delphy 1996: 37). For radical materialist feminism, then, as for Beauvoir, there is no essential or 'natural' femininity in language, in the body or anywhere else because femininity is defined and only exists within a social context.

FEMINIST CHALLENGES TO BEAUVOIR

Beauvoir's thinking on gender has been challenged for appearing to argue that women have no alternative but to become 'like men' if they want to live autonomously. She is accused of denying femininity, feminine activities and discounting women's difference. However, this is a misreading of Beauvoir's position, for, as we saw in Chapter 3, she does recognise the existence of certain biological differences between women and men, but does not accept that these differences are, in themselves, 'natural' or that biological differences should play a determining role in the elaboration of woman's subjectivity. Marriage and motherhood, as they are constituted in patriarchal society, entrap women in embodied immanence. For Beauvoir, the sexed body is a situation, a synthesis of facticity and freedom, not a biological fate.

Critics who interpret Beauvoir as arguing for women to be 'like men' in order to achieve autonomy are, more generally, sometimes taking issue with what they perceive as a residual Cartesian humanism seemingly apparent in Beauvoir's notion of sexed subjectivity. This interpretation of Beauvoir's analyses of gender is worth some discussion, as it neglects her innovative concept of 'situation' and consequently fails to see her relevance to recent postmodern feminisms. For example, Susan Hekman has noted (in a rather Sartrean reading of Beauvoir's intellectual project) an emphasis on the subject as singularly responsible for his or her actions and existence (Hekman 1990: 77–78):

> De Beauvoir's adherence to this unreconstructed Cartesian subject informs her particular variant of Enlightenment thought, existential humanism. It also exemplifies the errors of that epistemology in two fundamental ways. First, like the Enlightenment thinkers, she sees knowledge in the individualistic terms of the opposition of subject and object. At the root of her assertion that Self and Other are primordial categories is her belief that knowledge can only be acquired through the opposition of these two elements. Second, her acceptance of the Enlightenment dualism between subject and object means that she perpetuates the superiority of what the Enlightenment has defined as 'masculine' values.

> (Hekman 1990: 77)

Hekman is arguing here that the qualities that Beauvoir attributes to the subject, such as autonomy and rationality (characteristics of Descartes's notion of the subject, which has been prevalent since the seventeenth century), are those which have been traditionally constituted as masculine, so that, in *The Second Sex*, women are only offered a masculinised path to full subjecthood. Additionally, Hekman reads Beauvoir's analysis of gender as being rooted in the binary oppositions of self and Other, subject and object, which are themselves linchpins in Enlightenment systems of thought which have prevailed since the seventeenth century.

However, in opposition to these rather dualistic readings of Beauvoir's project, Sonia Kruks has argued that Beauvoir is, in fact, a pioneer in the attempt to reformulate the Cartesian subject (Kruks 1992). For Kruks, Beauvoir charts a middle course between essentialism and hyperconstructivism in her notion of subjectivity as 'situated'. It is precisely her use of the concept of 'situation' that enables her to avoid such dualistic thinking. But Beauvoir's close professional and personal association with Sartre and her positioning of Sartre as the creative impulse to *The Second Sex* may have fostered such early Sartrean readings of her text as Cartesian and humanist. Kruks points instead to the intersubjectivity of the subject in *The Second Sex* as 'both

THE ENLIGHTENMENT

The Enlightenment was an international movement of ideas which began in the late seventeenth century, inspired by the philosophy of René Descartes (1596–1650), and reached its peak in the mid eighteenth century. Enlightenment thinkers such as Jean-Jacques Rousseau (1712–1778), Immanuel Kant (1724–1804) and Hegel (see Chapter 1) emphasised reason, nature, logic and progress as the means of acquiring knowledge and safeguarding humanity's freedom. Enlightenment thinking conceptualised the human subject as coherent, stable, rational, unified and, in practice, as white and male. In the twentieth century, the Enlightenment legacy has been fundamentally challenged by feminism and postmodernism, particularly for its anthropocentric definitions of knowledge and selfhood.

constituting and constituted' and to the embodied aspect of woman's situation as two key insights in Beauvoir's view of the subject (Kruks 1992: 104–105).

Additionally, Moi has recently argued that Beauvoir's notion of the body as a situation is a crucially original and often overlooked contribution to feminist theory (Moi 1999: 59). She argues that the concept of 'situation' as a synthesis of facticity and freedom enables Beauvoir to avoid precisely having to divide lived experience up into the traditional subject–object binary (Moi 1999: 65). Moreover, as we saw in Chapters 2 and 3, the potential for reciprocal relations between self and Other is fundamental to Beauvoir's thinking, which, in any case, does not conceptualise the self–Other dynamic merely as a subject–object relation, but acknowledges the possibility of subject–subject relations.

Finally, in addition to her innovative use of the concept of 'situation', Beauvoir's foregrounding of the axiomatic question, 'What is a woman?', which underpins *The Second Sex*, has been most recently analysed in a bid to demonstrate how she rewrites the Cartesian subject from a feminist perspective (Bauer 2001: 46–77).

Another factor in misreadings and neglect of Beauvoir's work is that, during the 1970s and 1980s in parts of the Anglo-American academy, French feminism was conflated with differentialist, psychoanalytic feminism (Delphy 1995: 190–221). This assumption was based on some of the early anthologies and translations of French feminist thought published in the 1970s and 1980s, which misrepresented its diversity as an 'exotic' feminism uniquely rooted in psychoanalysis and French philosophy (Leonard and Adkins 1996: 3–9). This left Beauvoir's impact on feminist thinking rather out of the picture in certain parts of the academy, as her thought was inaccurately perceived to be associated with an earlier first-wave egalitarian feminism which was out of step with contemporary differentialist and postmodern feminisms in France. This relative neglect of Beauvoir's thought in some quarters has not been helped by the fact that the 1953 English translation of *The Second Sex* (upon which some translations into other languages were based) is incomplete, philosophically inaccurate and confusing (Simons 1999: 61–71). This factor has also facilitated reception of Beauvoir's work as less philosophically important than it undoubtedly is. It is indeed an intellectual tragedy that the philosophically original text that Beauvoir wrote is not the text that successive readers outside France and francophone countries have read!

RELEVANCE OF BEAUVOIR'S FEMINIST THOUGHT

It has been argued that one of the reasons why *The Second Sex* is still relevant to feminist debates today is 'because Beauvoir's understanding of the concept of power is remarkably modern' (Warren 1987: 40). Warren observes:

> Finding that its traditional forms fail to explain the male/female asymmetry, she [Beauvoir] turns her attention to the discourse and sets of practices which both constitute and execute gender relations in everyday life, that is, male power in practice. This, combined with her relentless account of 'becoming a woman' with its attendant internalization and playing out of Otherness, results in her astute analysis of the micro-politics of the constitution of self as female subject, as Other, in Western culture.
>
> (1987: 40)

On many occasions in *The Second Sex*, Beauvoir represents gender relations through the 'micro-politics' involved in the lived experience of everyday transactions in relationships. Power is not represented as monolithic and repressive or as the unique preserve of men in *The Second Sex*, but as a potential for action which, in most cases, can be grasped by either women or men. Warren identifies several themes in Beauvoir's text which have been developed (with or without explicit acknowledgement of her work) in various directions recently by a wide range of gender and cultural theorists.

Monique Wittig, for example, has provided a critique of hetero-sexuality as a political institution; the flawed repetition of gender as 'melancholic performance' has been developed by Judith Butler, who radically interprets Beauvoir's notion that 'One is not born, but rather becomes, a woman.' The relationship between sexed subjectivity and corporeality has been explored in, for example, French feminist revisions of psychoanalysis by Cixous, Irigaray, Sarah Kofman and Kristeva, among others. Moreover, Beauvoir's early feminist critique of classical psychoanalysis has been developed in different ways in an Anglophone context by Juliet Mitchell and Nancy Chodorow in the 1970s, as well as by French differentialist feminists.

It is appropriate, then, to consider briefly how some of these theo-rists have developed and contested certain aspects of Beauvoir's thought. Wittig and Delphy are perhaps the best known of French radical materialist feminists. Wittig's work is more well known than Delphy's because her literary writing has been widely translated. In 1992, some of Wittig's theoretical essays were translated in *The Straight Mind*, which brought her work to a wider English-speaking audience. Both Wittig and Delphy agree that there are no 'natural' categories of sex. In this, they broadly share Beauvoir's anti-naturalist view of gender – that no 'natural' gender exists. As Wittig argues in 'The category of sex', it is oppression which creates sexual difference (Wittig 1992: 2). Like Beauvoir, Wittig emphasises the inequality of power relations between women and men as crucial to an under-standing of sexual difference. Wittig, however, in a radical move away from Beauvoir's thinking, emphasises heterosexuality as the source of women's oppression, arguing that heterosexuality infuses everything, operating as a political institution which determines what can be said and done to the extent that its political operation is barely noticed. Wittig observes: 'Heterosexuality is always already there within all mental categories' (Wittig 1992: 43). The notion that heterosexuality operates as a political institution has also been explored by Adrienne Rich, who argued a similar if less radical position in her influential essay, 'Compulsory heterosexuality and lesbian existence' (Rich 1980: 631–660).

In the case of Delphy and Wittig, although there are some significant similarities between their thinking on sex, sexuality and gender, Delphy does not accept Wittig's claim that lesbians, as fugitives from the heterosexual social contract, are not women. Delphy sees gender, heterosexuality and homosexuality as culturally constructed (Jackson 1996: 136). Like Beauvoir, Delphy does not deny the existence of anatomical differences between women and men, but denies that these differences are socially significant in themselves (Jackson 1996: 142). As noted in Chapter 3, Beauvoir does not envisage the operation of heterosexuality or lesbianism in such a radical manner as Wittig or Rich. Moreover, Beauvoir and Wittig disagree over the social construction of sex or the view that anatomical sex differences are a product of patriarchal ideology rather than male and female biology (Gunther 1998: 180). As we have seen, Beauvoir views the division of the sexes as 'a biological fact, not an event in human history' (Beauvoir 1997: 19). Beauvoir, unlike Wittig, does not argue that both sex and gender should be dissolved into the neutral category of 'humanity' (Gunther 1998: 182).

Irigaray and Kristeva, however, have developed their work in rather different directions to Beauvoir, although both recognise the importance of her thought. Broadly linked with the differentialist tendency in second-wave French feminism of the 1970s, both Irigaray and Kristeva in their respective critiques of the Western philosophical tradition, psychoanalysis, language and culture have focused on issues of sexual difference and motherhood to a greater extent than Beauvoir. Both have tended to acknowledge yet distance themselves from her thinking on gender, associating her with an outmoded, egalitarian feminism (Irigaray 1995: 10; Kristeva in Rodgers 1998: 201).

Irigaray, like Beauvoir, rejects classical psychoanalysis as a conceptual framework for envisioning an authentic female subjectivity outside patriarchy. However, Irigaray and Beauvoir both recognise the importance of combining feminist theory and praxis to transform the situation of women and advocate a sexed equality with men (Gunther 1998: 186). Although they conceptualise women's liberation differently, Beauvoir and Irigaray agree that the subject in patriarchal society is exclusively male (Schor 1989: 43). Yet it can be argued that Irigaray's critique of the phallogocentrism (patriarchal symbolic system) of Western metaphysics is more radical than Beauvoir's in that she rejects the notion that woman's difference can be represented at all in patriarchal signifying systems. This is at odds with Beauvoir's position, for she believed in transforming patriarchy and its signifying systems from within.

Kristeva, however, critical of egalitarian feminisms (with which she associates Beauvoir) and of essentialising notions of femininity associated with differentialist feminisms, has been concerned with sexual differentiation in subjectivity and the valorisation of the maternal, drawing on a Freudian psychoanalytic framework, semiotics and Derridean deconstruction. These theoretical preoccupations distance her considerably from Beauvoir's thought, despite the fact that she recognises her as a powerful intellectual role model for women, dedicating her recent work on female genius, *Le Génie féminin*, to Beauvoir (Kristeva 1999–2002).

BEAUVOIR AND BUTLER

Since the publication of *Gender Trouble* in 1990, Judith Butler has come to be seen as perhaps the most influential contemporary theorist of gender. In that text, she develops Beauvoir's notion of 'becoming woman' in radical directions. In an earlier pre-*Gender Trouble* article on Beauvoir, which is essential reading to understand Butler's debt to Beauvoir, Butler explored the radical possibilities of dismantling the relationship between sex, gender and sexuality in the context of Beauvoir's discussion of the body as 'situation' (Butler 1986: 35–49). Butler radically argues that, 'if a pure body cannot be found, if what can be found is the situated body, locus of cultural interpretations, then Simone de Beauvoir's theory seems implicitly to ask whether sex was not gender all along' (Butler 1986: 46). Butler sees Beauvoir's account of the body as an 'interpretive modality' as being useful for understanding the ways in which we perform bodily acts of gender, which are then interpreted within the cultural field as conforming to or contesting particular conventions governing sex and gender.

Butler develops these notions within a broader theoretical framework in *Gender Trouble*. Her aim in this text is to deconstruct the ontology or apparent 'fact' of gender and to explore how gender identity is enforced by a melancholic, repetitive performance of acts of gender which together solidify into 'gender' as an essential, 'natural' facet of selfhood. She argues, for example, that there need not be a doer or agent behind the deed or act of gender 'performance', but rather that the doer is constructed in and through the deed of gender. That is to say that we become gendered beings through the acts of gender that we perform, rather than vice versa. For example, if a woman always dresses in a mini-skirt and high heels, she is repeatedly conforming to a particular dress code which, since the 1960s, has re-inforced traditional notions of heterosexual femininity (signalling, for example, constrained physical mobility or passivity and sexual avail-ability to heterosexual men). But at the same time, traditional notions of heterosexual masculinity are also being reinforced in this instance as men are expected to respond to this dress code by registering the interpretations of gender and sexuality in play. In this way, similar per-formances of gender, through their perpetual repetition, produce sexed categories which become reified into gender norms, according to Butler. It is when these norms are contested, for example, when a man wears high heels and a mini-skirt, that gender and sexuality begin to reveal themselves as potentially fictive, temporary identities or performances. In elaborating this radical view of gender, Butler is trying to liberate feminism from what she sees as the static essentialism involved in its self-constitution as a foundational identity politics. In other words, she is seeking to dislodge the restrictive notions of gender which are themselves implicit in feminism's political project, rooted as it is in particular notions of femininity. Butler proposes that, if identity is viewed as the product of feminism's discourse rather than its origin, feminism can address itself to subverting the ways in which that identity is produced and repeated. In short, if we view the doer of gender as constructed through the deed of gender, we can start to envisage different ways of reconstructing that doer.

Space constraints prevent us from considering extensively Butler's indebtedness to Beauvoir's thinking. But we can note initially, with Moi, that the notion of 'performing' one's gender has affinities with existen-tialism's emphasis on action (Moi 1999: 55). Both Beauvoir and Butler are anti-essentialist, interested in the 'becoming' of gender. But Butler sees gender identity as an effect of oppressive power relations, as a regulatory fiction. As Moi says, 'for Beauvoir women exist, for Butler, they have to be deconstructed' (Moi 1999: 76). Moreover, as noted above, in *The Second Sex* Beauvoir is interested in the dynamics of power and the lived experience of gender rather than in identity itself, entail-ing that she focuses on situated subjectivity in its continually elaborated relations with others, the body, time, etc. (Moi 1999: 81).

It is intriguing to wonder what Beauvoir would have made of Butler's original syntheses of thinking on sex and gender. It is likely that she would have rejected what some have seen as Butler's early anti-materialism and her focus on the reification of gender identities; for Beauvoir, as for Delphy and Wittig, the category of 'women' is a social and material reality, subject to structural inequalities in patriarchal society (Jackson 1996: 137–138). Moreover, Beauvoir 'refuses to hand the concept of "woman" over to the opposition' (Moi 1999: 77), seeking to provide a phenomenological analysis of the concrete reality of woman's existence. Indeed, it has been argued that Butler fails to integrate Beauvoir's phenomenological understanding of the body (as a dynamic lived experience) into her discussion, revealing her (Butler's) own investment in the sex/gender distinction (Heinämaa 1997; Moi 1999: 72–74).

Finally, in this brief overview of Beauvoir's legacy in gender studies, it is worth noting that academic, media and biographical representations of Beauvoir herself have been the focus of a study devoted to an analysis of the discursive production of bisexuality and the ways in which it disrupts notions of identity (Fraser 1999). Such an analysis of the cultural production of 'Simone de Beauvoir' as an identity formation indicates her continuing legacy as both an iconoclastic cultural icon and thinker.

BEAUVOIR'S BROADER LEGACY

We have mainly focused thus far on *The Second Sex* and its continuing relevance to recent debates in feminist theory and philosophy; however, its impact can also be traced in postcolonial studies, among other disciplines. Moi, for example, has argued that *The Second Sex* is a likely major influence on Frantz Fanon's groundbreaking *Black Skin, White Masks*, published in 1952, only three years after Beauvoir's study of women (Moi 1994: 204–207). Like Beauvoir, Fanon (1925–1961) – considered by many to be the founder of postcolonial studies – draws on Hegelian philosophy, Sartrean existentialism, anthropology and psychoanalysis to theorise black embodied alienation in a racist society. Heavily influenced by Sartre and an avid reader of *Les Temps Modernes* in the late 1940s, Fanon is likely to have come across extracts from *The Second Sex* which appeared in the journal, although surprisingly there is no mention of Beauvoir's study in *Black Skin, White Masks*. Moreover,

Beauvoir makes explicit connections between aspects of the oppression of Jews, blacks and women in *The Second Sex* which encourage a post-colonial engagement with her work (Mianda 2001; Tidd 2002).

In feminist history, developing the extensive historical analyses of *The Second Sex* (regrettably a section abridged in the English translation of the text), historians such as Gerda Lerner, Sheila Rowbotham, Geneviève Fraisse and Michèle Perrot, among others, have continued Beauvoir's work, seeking to challenge patriarchal methods of historical analysis and the absence of women in historical accounts.

Elsewhere in feminist critiques of science, Evelyn Fox Keller, Sarah Hrdy and others have developed Beauvoir's analyses of biology in *The Second Sex* in new directions (Fallaize in O'Brien and Embree 2001).

In feminist literary criticism and practice, Beauvoir's chapters of literary criticism in *The Second Sex* and her own fictional and auto/biographical texts were precursors of the wealth of feminist criticism and writing available today. In the case of feminist literary criticism, Beauvoir's work was initially continued outside France – although without her specifically mythological analysis – by the Anglo-American 'Images of women' critics in the early 1970s, such as Mary Ellmann, Kate Millet and Germaine Greer, who studied the use of female stereotypes in male writing. In terms of textual practice, in France, an obvious inheritor of Beauvoir's legacy is the school of 1970s' 'new realism' in French women's writing, specifically Annie Ernaux and Claire Etcherelli.

Elsewhere in feminist cultural criticism, Beauvoir's analysis of woman as 'Other' and as object of the male gaze can be traced in film studies, in the influential work of Laura Mulvey (Mulvey 1975). Mulvey has used Lacanian psychoanalysis to analyse gendered spectator positions in a feminist critique of Hollywood cinema. She shows how pleasure in looking has been split between an active male looker and passive female object of the gaze. Traditional films present men as active, controlling subjects and position women as passive objects of desire for men in both the film's narrative and in their roles as spectators in the audience. Traditional films do not allow women to be active desiring sexual subjects in their own right, either on screen or in the audience. Such films consequently objectify women in relation to a dominating 'male gaze', presenting 'woman as image' or 'spectacle' and man as 'bearer of the look'. So it is men who do the looking; women are there to be *looked at*. Aspects of Mulvey's analyses of gender and film spectatorship develop Beauvoir's early analyses of the politics of the male gaze in *The Second Sex* and in her essay on Brigitte Bardot, which itself constitutes an early example of feminist film criticism.

Further afield, in feminist theology, the influence of Beauvoir's study of women is also recognised, for example by the radical feminist theologian, Mary Daly (1928–) in *The Church and the Second Sex* (1968). Although Daly notes that Beauvoir is not specifically concerned with the Church, she identifies Beauvoir's critique of Catholic ideology and practice in relation to the situation of women in *The Second Sex* and elsewhere in her fiction and memoirs as an important early influence in feminist theology.

Despite this brief overview, the multi-disciplinary scope of Beauvoir's influence is hard to quantify and sometimes is not acknowledged explicitly, as new syntheses in thinking are made and acknowledgement of earlier influences is lost. Currently, in Beauvoir studies, there is a renaissance of interest in her philosophical thought. Her literary writings, her ethical essays and *Old Age* have (in conjunction with *The Second Sex*) been the focus of recent and forthcoming rereadings, some of which seek to trace her phenomenological, feminist and more general philosophical preoccupations throughout her writings (Bauer 2001; Bergoffen 1997; Fallaize 1998; Fullbrook and Fullbrook 1998; Lundgren-Gothlin 1996; Mahon 1997; O'Brien and Embree 2001; Tidd 1999). Moreover, there is a major project, *The Beauvoir Series*, currently under way to publish her previously untranslated writings, some of which are discussed in this study (Simons and Le Bon de Beauvoir forthcoming). Regrettably, *The Second Sex* has not yet been retranslated into English and, consequently, the 1953 edited translation by H. M. Parshley, with its philosophical inconsistencies and omissions, is still the only version available.

Simone de Beauvoir's stature as a leading critical thinker remains assured and subject to lively ongoing debate. Suffice it to say, interest in her thought is thriving across the world as new generations of readers engage with the 'emblematic intellectual woman of the twentieth century' (Moi 1994: 1).

FURTHER READING

This list is divided into several sections: the first contains annotated bibliographical references to most of Simone de Beauvoir's published works in French and in English as relevant to this study. Although most of her work is translated into English, some of these translations are incomplete, philosophically inaccurate and dated, particularly in the case of Beauvoir's major work, *The Second Sex*. For information on the shortcomings of the English translation, see Simons' 1983 article reprinted in Simons (1999: 61–71). Readers are consequently advised to read Beauvoir's texts in the original French where possible. In a major project, *The Beauvoir Series*, edited by Margaret Simons and Sylvie Le Bon de Beauvoir (forthcoming from University of Illinois Press), some of Beauvoir's texts are currently being either translated for the first time or retranslated, accompanied by critical introductions by leading figures in Beauvoir studies. This will enable readers to access recent English translations of many of her key texts, some of which were previously only available in French. The second section of this list contains annotated references to some of Beauvoir's major interviews, which are often accessible ways of understanding key aspects of her thought. The final section provides a list of key critical works on Beauvoir's philosophical and literary writing. Some of these titles are not available in English, but are nevertheless referenced for the reader's information. In addition to this 'Further Reading' bibliography, readers

are encouraged to consult three additional comprehensive sources
of bibliographical information on Beauvoir's work, detailed below:
Francis and Gontier (1979), Bennett and Hochmann (1988) and
O'Brien and Embree (2001).

BOOKS AND SHORT TEXTS BY SIMONE DE BEAUVOIR

PHILOSOPHY, POLITICS, TRAVEL

Beauvoir, Simone de (1944) *Pyrrhus et Cinéas*, Paris: Gallimard 'Idées'.
    Beauvoir's first existentialist essay; analyses transcendence, the self-
other relation and situation. Currently being translated.

—— (1945) 'La *Phénoménologie de la Perception*', *Les Temps Modernes* 2:
363–367.
    Review of Merleau-Ponty's *Phenomenology of Perception*; useful for
identifying theoretical proximities between Beauvoir and Merleau-
Ponty.

—— (1947) *Pour une morale de l'ambiguïté*, Paris: Gallimard. (Trans.
Bernard Frechtman, *The Ethics of Ambiguity* (1994), New York: Citadel
Press.)
    Existentialist ethics, rooted in the notion of ambiguity. Important
for its discussion of freedom and situation, especially as later developed
in *The Second Sex*.

—— (1948) *L'Existentialisme et la sagesse des nations*, Paris: Nagel.
    Comprises four short essays: 'L'Existentialisme et la sagesse des
nations' (a defence of existentialism); 'Idéalisme et réalisme et politique' (discussion of relationship between means and ends, ethics and
politics); 'Littérature et métaphysique' (discussion of the metaphysical
novel); and 'Oeil pour oeil' (discussion of revenge and justice in the
French context of the post-Libération period).

—— (1949) '*Les Structures élémentaires de la parenté*', *Les Temps Modernes*
5 (49): 943–949.
    Review of Lévi-Strauss's *Elementary Structures of Kinship*; useful for
identifying theoretical proximities between Beauvoir and Lévi-Strauss.

—— (1949) *Le Deuxième Sexe, Vol 1: Les Faits et les mythes; Vol 2: L'Expérience vécue*, Paris: Gallimard. (Trans. and ed. H. M. Parshley, *The Second Sex* (1953), London: Jonathan Cape; reissued 1977, London: Vintage.)

Essential reading. Beauvoir's groundbreaking study of the situation of women from prehistory to the late 1940s. Introduces the pioneering concepts of woman as the absolute Other and of 'becoming woman'. Tackling *The Second Sex* in any language might seem a daunting task, although, compared to many theoretical texts, it is in fact very clear and readable. If time is limited, readers can concentrate on the Introduction and Section I in the first volume and on the second volume. The well-known (but clumsily translated) phrase, 'one is not born, but rather becomes, a woman', opens the first chapter of Part IV. The English translation is incomplete and sometimes philosophically incorrect in its terminological use, so refer to the French original where possible.

—— (1954) *L'Amérique au jour le jour*, Paris: Gallimard. (Trans. C. Cosman, *America Day By Day* (1998), London: Victor Gollancz.)

Travel diary record of Beauvoir's four-month trip to America in 1947; provides an intellectual's understanding of the American national psyche through its culture and customs, attentive to the situation of women and the black population. Interesting but not essential reading.

—— (1955) *Privilèges*, Paris: Gallimard. (Trans. A. Michelson, *Must We Burn Sade?* (1953), London: Peter Nevill; trans. V. Zaytzeff and F. Morrison, 'Merleau-Ponty and pseudo-sartreanism' (1989), *International Studies in Philosophy* 21: 3–48.)

Comprises three essays: 'Faut-il brûler Sade?' originally published in 1951–1952 in *Les Temps Modernes* (discussion of life and work of the Marquis de Sade; outlines briefly an ethics of the erotic); 'La pensée de droite, aujourd'hui' (a critique of right-wing thought); and 'Merleau-Ponty et le pseudo-sartrisme' (a defence of Sartre's thought against Merleau-Ponty's 1955 critique in *Les Aventures de la dialectique* of Sartre's ultrabolshevism).

—— (1957) *La Longue Marche: Essai sur la Chine*, Paris: Gallimard. (Trans. A. Wainhouse, *The Long March: An Account of Modern China* (1958), London: Deutsch/Weidenfeld and Nicolson.)

Book-length portrait of China in the mid 1950s, based on Beauvoir's visit to the country in 1955. Useful snapshot of Beauvoir's political views in the 1950s, but not essential reading.

—— (1962) *Djamila Boupacha*, with Gisèle Halimi, Paris: Gallimard. (Trans. P. Green, *Djamila Boupacha* (1962), London: Deutsch/ Weidenfeld and Nicolson.)

Preface by Beauvoir and collection of documents relevant to case of Djamila Boupacha, an Algerian woman tortured by French soldiers during the Algerian War of 1954–1962. Early example of Beauvoir's interventionist politics, but not essential reading.

—— (1970) *La Vieillesse*. Paris: Gallimard. (Trans. P. O'Brien, *Old Age* (1977), Harmondsworth: Penguin.)

Wide-ranging study of ageing in Western societies, from the perspectives of biology, anthropology, history and sociology and as experienced internally by old people.

—— (1979) 'Brigitte Bardot et le syndrome de Lolita', in C. Francis and F. Gontier (eds) *Les Ecrits de Simone de Beauvoir*, Paris: Gallimard, pp. 363–376. (Trans. B. Frechtman, *Brigitte Bardot and the Lolita Syndrome* (1960), London: Deutsch/Weidenfeld and Nicolson.)

Mythological critique of Brigitte Bardot as an example of 'the eternal feminine' and as subversive erotic figure.

—— (1979) 'Situation de la femme aujourd'hui', in C. Francis and F. Gontier (eds) *Les Ecrits de Simone de Beauvoir*, Paris: Gallimard, pp. 422–438.

One of three lectures delivered in Japan; a useful snapshot of Beauvoir's views on women's situation in the 1960s and why feminism is necessary.

—— (1979) 'Solidaire d'Israël: un soutien critique', in C. Francis and F. Gontier (eds) *Les Ecrits de Simone de Beauvoir*, Paris: Gallimard, pp. 522–532.

Lecture explaining Beauvoir's pro-Israel stance. Useful background for those interested in her politics.

FICTION AND DRAMA

Beauvoir, Simone de (1943) *L'Invitée*, Paris: Gallimard. (Trans. Y. Moyse and R. Senhouse, *She Came to Stay* (1975), Glasgow: Fontana/Collins; originally published 1949.)

Beauvoir's first published novel focusing on a triangular relationship between two women and one man. A fictional illustration of the conflictual aspects of the self–Other relationship, it provides examples of existentialist concepts, such as 'being-for-oneself', 'being-for-others', 'the look of the Other', 'shame' and 'anguish'.

—— (1945) *Le Sang des autres*, Paris: Gallimard. (Trans. Y. Moyse and R. Senhouse, *The Blood of Others* (1964), Harmondsworth: Penguin; originally published 1948.)

Fictional companion to *Pyrrhus et Cinéas*; set in Resistance France, the novel deals with ethical dilemmas relating to action, responsibility and freedom.

—— (1945) *Les Bouches inutiles*, Paris: Gallimard. (Trans. C. Francis and F. Gontier, *The Useless Mouths* (1983), Florissant, MO: River Press; new trans. C. Naji and L. Stanley, Urbana, IL: University of Illinois Press, forthcoming.)

Beauvoir's only piece of theatre, dealing with issues of freedom, responsibility and gender politics, set in a superficially medieval commune.

—— (1946) *Tous les hommes sont mortels*, Paris: Gallimard. (Trans. E. Cameron and L. M. Friedman, *All Men are Mortal* (1995), London: Virago.)

Historical novel dealing with philosophical themes of mortality, action, commitment and responsibility through the dilemmas of the central character, Fosca, who is condemned to be immortal. Constitutes an implicit fictional critique of Hegel's abstract universalism by affirming the value of situated collective and committed human projects.

—— (1954) *Les Mandarins*, Paris: Gallimard. (Trans. L. M. Friedman, *The Mandarins* (1957), London and Glasgow: Collins.)

Goncourt Prize-winning novel, set in post-Liberation France, in which individual and collective ethical dilemmas are played out against the backdrop of cold war politics. An important portrait of the situation of intellectuals in this period, the novel explores the political and personal exigencies which impinge on the possibilities of action, authenticity and truth-telling.

—— (1966) *Les Belles Images*, Paris: Gallimard. (Trans. P. O'Brian, *Les Belles Images* (1968), London and Glasgow: Collins.)

Novel set amid the affluent, technocratic Parisian bourgeoisie of the 1960s, focusing on women's alienated situation in patriarchal society.

—— (1968) *La Femme rompue*, Paris: Gallimard. (Trans. P. O'Brian, *The Woman Destroyed* (1969), London and Glasgow: Collins.)

Three short stories, focusing on women's alienated situation and their relationship to language.

—— (1979) *Quand prime le spirituel*, Paris: Gallimard. (Trans. P. O'Brian, *When Things of the Spirit Come First* (1982), London: Deutsch/Weidenfeld and Nicolson.)

Early collection of five short stories, originally written in the 1930s, exploring young women's experiences of bourgeois Catholic ideology.

—— (1979) 'Deux chapitres inédits de *L'Invitée*', in C. Francis and F. Gontier (eds) *Les Ecrits de Simone de Beauvoir*, Paris: Gallimard, pp. 275–316. (Translation forthcoming, University of Illinois Press.)

Two previously unpublished chapters to *L'Invitée* (*She Came to Stay*), excised from the novel, focusing on Françoise's childhood and sexuality.

—— (1992) 'Malentendu à Moscou', *Roman 20–50 'Simone de Beauvoir'* 13: 137–188.

Short story omitted from *La Femme rompue* (*The Woman Destroyed*), dealing with the dilemmas of a retired couple and containing material on the Soviet Union in the mid 1960s.

ON LITERATURE

Beauvoir, Simone de (1965) Contribution to 'Que peut la littérature?' debate, in Yves Buin (ed.) *Que peut la littérature?* Paris: Union générale d'éditions, pp. 73–92.

Key statement on Beauvoir's view of the role of literature analysed in Chapter 5 of this volume. Read it if you can get hold of it.

—— (1979a) 'Mon expérience d'écrivain', in C. Francis and F. Gontier (eds) *Les Ecrits de Simone de Beauvoir*, Paris: Gallimard, pp. 439–457.

One of several lectures given by Beauvoir in Japan in 1966; important statement on writing, especially the roles of fiction and autobiography, analysed in Chapter 5 of this volume. Recommended.

—— (1979b) 'La femme et la création' in C. Francis and F. Gontier (eds) *Les Ecrits de Simone de Beauvoir*, Paris: Gallimard, pp. 458–474. (Trans. R. Mallaghan, 'Women and creativity' in T. Moi (ed.) *French Feminist Thought* (1987), Oxford: Blackwell, pp. 17–31.)

Analysis of women's relationship to creativity in patriarchal society, analysed in Chapter 5 of this volume. Recommended.

AUTO/BIOGRAPHY

Beauvoir, Simone de (1958) *Mémoires d'une jeune fille rangée*, Paris: Gallimard. (Trans. J. Kirkup, *Memoirs of a Dutiful Daughter* (1963), Harmondsworth: Penguin.)

First volume of Beauvoir's autobiography, covering the years 1908–1929 and illustrating elements of her philosophical thought. All four volumes of autobiography are useful reading in acquiring a detailed understanding of Beauvoir's intellectual project.

—— (1960) *La Force de l'âge*, Paris: Gallimard. (Trans. P. Green, *The Prime of Life* (1965), Harmondsworth, Penguin.)

Second volume of autobiography, covering the period 1929–1944.

—— (1963) *La Force des choses I et II*, Paris: Gallimard. (Trans. R. Howard, *Force of Circumstance* (1968), Harmondsworth: Penguin.)

Third volume of autobiography, spanning the period of 1944–1962.

—— (1964) *Une Mort très douce*. Paris: Gallimard. (Trans. P. O'Brian, *A Very Easy Death* (1969), Harmondsworth: Penguin.)

Short biographical testimony to the illness and death of Françoise de Beauvoir, illustrating several existentialist concepts.

—— (1972) *Tout compte fait*. Paris: Gallimard. (Trans. P. O'Brian, *All Said and Done* (1977), Harmondsworth: Penguin.)

Final volume of autobiography, organised thematically, covering the period 1962–1972.

—— (1981) *La Cérémonie des adieux*, suivi de *Entretiens avec Jean-Paul Sartre*, Paris: Gallimard. (Trans. P. O'Brian, *Adieux: A Farewell to Sartre* (1985), Harmondsworth: Penguin.)

The first part relates the last ten years of Sartre's life, 1970–1980; the second much longer section comprises a series of interviews with Sartre conducted by Beauvoir in 1974.

—— (1990) *Journal de guerre*. Paris: Gallimard.

Beauvoir's posthumously published diary of life in occupied Paris during the Second World War, edited by her adopted daughter, Sylvie Le Bon de Beauvoir. Useful background reading.

—— (1990) *Lettres à Sartre I, 1930–1939*; *II, 1940–1963*, Paris: Gallimard. (Trans. Q. Hoare, *Letters to Sartre* (1991), London: Radius.)

Posthumously published correspondence with Sartre, edited by Sylvie Le Bon de Beauvoir, covering the period of many of Beauvoir's major publications; valuable intellectual and personal portrait. Useful background reading.

—— (1998) *Beloved Chicago Man, Letters to Nelson Algren 1947–64*, London: Gollancz. (Trans. S. Le Bon de Beauvoir, *Lettres à Nelson Algren, un amour transatlantique 1947–64* (1997), Paris: Gallimard.)

Correspondence with US social realist writer, Nelson Algren, providing important cultural and political commentary on France in the cold war years. A good background read.

INTERVIEWS

Beauvoir, Simone de (1966) 'Entretiens avec Simone de Beauvoir' in F. Jeanson, *Simone de Beauvoir ou l'entreprise de vivre*, Paris: Seuil, pp. 258–291.

Two very useful interviews (in French) focusing on aspects of *The Second Sex*, feminism more generally and Beauvoir's autobiographical project.

—— (1976) '*The Second Sex*: 25 years later', *Society* 13 (2): 79–85. (Trans. '*Le Deuxième Sexe*, vingt-cinq ans après', in C. Francis and F. Gontier (eds) *Les Ecrits de Simone de Beauvoir*, Paris: Gallimard, pp. 547–565.)

As its title suggests, an overview of the issues raised in *The Second Sex*; useful for an understanding of how Beauvoir's feminism evolved during the second-wave feminist period.

—— (1979c) 'Entretien avec Simone de Beauvoir', in C. Francis and F. Gontier (eds) *Les Ecrits de Simone de Beauvoir*, Paris: Gallimard, pp. 583–592.

Discussion about *The Second Sex* and Beauvoir's impact on the development of feminism; interesting but not essential.

—— (1979d) 'Interview with Simone de Beauvoir', *Signs: Journal of Women in Culture and Society* 5: 224–236.

Important interview with US academic, Alice Jardine, in which Beauvoir talks about psychoanalysis, women's writing, autobiography and language.

—— (1979) 'Une interview de Simone de Beauvoir par Madeleine Chapsal', in C. Francis and F. Gontier (eds) *Les Ecrits de Simone de Beauvoir*, Paris: Gallimard, pp. 381–396.

Wide-ranging interview covering much of Beauvoir's work, including *The Second Sex* and her literary writings.

—— (1984) *Simone de Beauvoir aujourd'hui: Entretiens*, Paris: Mercure de France. (Trans. M. Howarth, *Simone de Beauvoir Today: Conversations 1972–82* (1984), London: Chatto and Windus, The Hogarth Press.)

Set of six interviews with German feminist journalist, Alice Schwarzer, focusing mainly on *The Second Sex* and the development of Beauvoir's feminism. Essential reading.

—— (1999) Three interviews, in M. A. Simons *Beauvoir and The Second Sex, Feminism, Race and the Origins of Existentialism*, Lanham and Oxford: Rowman and Littlefield, pp. 1–21, 55–59, 93–100.

Wide-ranging interviews tackling Beauvoir's influence on Sartre; her training and role as a philosopher; current issues in feminism in relation to *The Second Sex*; and the Parshley translation of *The Second Sex*.

WORKS ON SIMONE DE BEAUVOIR

JOURNALS

In addition to the works cited below, readers are encouraged to consult *Simone de Beauvoir Studies*, a journal established in 1983, based in North America, and published by the International Simone de Beauvoir Society, which also runs an annual conference devoted to Beauvoir's work. You can contact the International Simone de Beauvoir Society c/o Professor Yolanda Astarita Patterson, 440 La Mesa Drive, Menlo Park, CA 94028–97455, USA, or via the web site at http://www.simonedebeauvoir.free.fr.

Kail, Michel (ed.) (2002) 'Présences de Simone de Beauvoir', *Les Temps Modernes* 619.

Special issue of journal comprising an interview and eleven articles on Beauvoir's thought. Recommended.

Simons, Margaret A. (ed.) (1999) 'The Philosophy of Simone de Beauvoir', *Hypatia: A Journal of Feminist Philosophy* 14 (4).

Essays on diverse aspects of Beauvoir's philosophy and its influence on her literary writing. Recommended.

Wenzel, Hélène V. (ed.) (1986) 'Simone de Beauvoir: Witness to a Century', *Yale French Studies* 72.

Important collection of essays on a range of Beauvoir's philosophical and literary writing, including one by Judith Butler.

BOOKS AND ARTICLES

Al-Hibri, Azizah Y. and Simons, Margaret A. (eds) (1990) *Hypatia Reborn: Essay in Feminist Philosophy*, Bloomington and Indianapolis: Indiana University Press.

Part Three contains nine essays on Beauvoir's feminist philosophy, including topics such as biology, lesbianism and embodiment in *The Second Sex*. Recommended.

Bair, Deirdre (1990) *Simone de Beauvoir,* London: Jonathan Cape.

Extensive biography.

Bauer, Nancy (2001) *Simone de Beauvoir: Philosophy and Feminism*, New York: Columbia University Press.

Important, clear and sophisticated study of *The Second Sex* and of Beauvoir's philosophical relationship to Descartes, Hegel and Sartre.

Bennett, Joy and Hochmann, Gabriella (1988) *Simone de Beauvoir: An Annotated Bibliography,* New York and London: Garland Publishing.

Extensive bibliography of works by and on Beauvoir published before 1988.

Bergoffen, Deborah (1997) *The Philosophy of Simone de Beauvoir: Gendered Phenomenologies, Erotic Generosities,* New York: SUNY.

Phenomenological study of Beauvoir's ethical essays, *The Second Sex* and *Old Age* in context of Sartre and Merleau-Ponty. Quite advanced for non-philosophers.

Butler, Judith (1986) 'Sex and gender in Simone de Beauvoir's *Second Sex*', in Hélène Wenzel (ed.) 'Simone de Beauvoir: Witness to a Century', *Yale French Studies* 72: 35–49.
  Important and accessible essay by a major gender theorist, providing a radical interpretation of Beauvoir's concept of 'becoming woman' through the notion of gender as construct and process, subsequently developed in a wider theoretical framework in Butler's groundbreaking *Gender Trouble* (1990). Essential, accessible reading for both Beauvoir and Butler enthusiasts.

Card, Claudia (ed.) (2003) *The Cambridge Companion to Simone de Beauvoir*, Cambridge: Cambridge University Press.
  Comprises fourteen essays by feminist philosophers and theorists examining major aspects of Beauvoir's thought, such as the relationship between gender and biology, sexuality and sexual difference and the influence of Heidegger, Husserl, Sartre and Merleau-Ponty on her work. Essential reading.

Coderre, Cécile and Tahon, Marie-Blanche (eds) (2001) *Le Deuxième Sexe: Une relecture en trois temps, 1949–1971–1999*, Montreal: Editions du Remue-Ménage.
  Wide-ranging collection of essays seeking to assess the contribution of *The Second Sex* to second-wave feminist debates.

Dayan, Josée and Ribowska, Malka (1979) *Simone de Beauvoir: Un film*, Paris: Gallimard.
  Filmscript of documentary film made about Beauvoir's life. Useful background material.

Delphy, Christine and Chaperon, Sylvie (eds) (2002) *Cinquantenaire du Deuxième Sexe*, Paris: Syllepse.
  Selected conference proceedings of the fiftieth anniversary conference of the French publication of *The Second Sex*, comprising over 60 articles addressing issues relating to Beauvoir's philosophy, and the reception and translation of her 1949 study.

Evans, Mary (1985) *Simone de Beauvoir: A Feminist Mandarin*, London: Tavistock.

Feminist sociological study of Beauvoir's theoretical and fictional texts. Accessible, although a little dated.

—— (1996) *Simone de Beauvoir*, London: Sage.

Introductory study of Beauvoir's life and writing. Accessible.

Evans, Ruth (ed.) (1998) *Simone de Beauvoir's The Second Sex: New Interdisciplinary Essays*, Manchester: Manchester University Press.

Collection of six interdisciplinary essays rereading *The Second Sex* for current generations of feminist readers. Important, accessible and worth the read.

Fallaize, Elizabeth (1988) *The Novels of Simone de Beauvoir*, London: Routledge.

Feminist study of Beauvoir's fiction, with particular focus on narrative strategies. Remains one of the best studies of Beauvoir's fiction. Essential reading.

—— (1998) *Simone de Beauvoir: A Critical Reader*, London/New York: Routledge.

Collection of key essays on Beauvoir's philosophy, fiction and autobiography. Essential reading.

Fishwick, Sarah (2002) *The Body in the Work of Simone de Beauvoir*, Oxford and New York: Peter Lang.

An introduction to Beauvoir's writings on corporeality.

Forster, Penny and Sutton, Imogen (eds) (1989) *Daughters of de Beauvoir*, London: The Women's Press and Arts Council (transcript of film).

Interviews with leading Anglo-American second-wave feminists, Beauvoir's adopted daughter, Sylvie Le Bon de Beauvoir, and sister, Hélène de Beauvoir, concerning the impact of Beauvoir's work.

Francis, Claude and Gontier, Fernande (eds) (1979) *Les Ecrits de Simone de Beauvoir*, Paris: Gallimard.

Invaluable bibliography, biography and collection of short previously unpublished texts by Beauvoir. Essential reading.

Fullbrook, Kate and Fullbrook, Edward (1993) *Simone de Beauvoir and Jean-Paul Sartre: The Remaking of a Twentieth Century Legend*, Hemel Hempstead: Harvester Wheatsheaf.

Largely biographical re-evaluation of the intellectual partnership of Beauvoir and Sartre, arguing that Beauvoir had a considerably greater philosophical influence on Sartre and existentialism than has been previously claimed.

―― (1998) *Simone de Beauvoir: A Critical Introduction*, Cambridge: Polity.

Introduction to Beauvoir's philosophical thought; focuses on main theoretical writings and provides philosophical readings of the fiction.

Gothlin, Eva (1997) 'Simone de Beauvoir's Ethics and its relation to current moral philosophy', *Simone de Beauvoir Studies* 14: 39–46.

Article focusing on Beauvoir's ethics of ambiguity and its relation to contemporary feminist moral philosophy, with reference to the ethics of Seyla Benhabib.

Gothlin, Eva (1999) 'Simone de Beauvoir's notions of appeal, desire and ambiguity, and their relationship to Jean-Paul Sartre's notions of appeal and desire' in *Hypatia Special Issue 'The Philosophy of Simone de Beauvoir'* 14 (4): 83–95.

Valuable and clear analysis of ambiguity, desire and appeal in Beauvoir's philosophy.

Gunther, Renate (1998) 'Fifty years on: the impact of Simone de Beauvoir's *Le Deuxième Sexe* on contemporary feminist theory', *Modern and Contemporary France* 6 (2): 177–188.

Clear discussion of the relationship between Beauvoir and Monique Wittig's materialist feminism; argues for a reassessment of the apparent opposition between Beauvoir's largely materialist position and Irigaray's differentialist feminism.

Heath, Jane (1989) *Simone de Beauvoir*, Brighton: Harvester Wheatsheaf.

Sophisticated study of some of Beauvoir's fiction, drawing on feminist psychoanalytic theory. Recommended.

Heinämaa, Sara (1997) 'What is a woman? Butler and Beauvoir on the foundations of sexual difference', *Hypatia* 12 (1): 20–39.

Article arguing that *The Second Sex* should be read as a phenomenological description of sexual difference.

Jeanson, Francis (1966) *Simone de Beauvoir ou l'entreprise de vivre*, Paris: Seuil.

Important early study of Beauvoir's writing project, focusing particularly on her autobiography.

Keefe, Terry (1983) *Simone de Beauvoir: A Study of her Writings*, Totowa, NJ: Barnes and Noble.
Solid, accessible introduction to Beauvoir's writing.

Kruks, Sonia (1990) *Situation and Human Existence: Freedom, Subjectivity and Society*, London: Unwin Hyman.
Important study of Beauvoir's philosophy, focusing on situation, freedom and subjectivity, and on the relationship between the philosophies of Beauvoir, Merleau-Ponty and Sartre. Essential reading.

—— (1992) 'Gender and subjectivity: Simone de Beauvoir and contemporary feminism', *Signs* 18 (1): 89–110.
Article arguing that Beauvoir's notion of the 'situated subject' is highly relevant to current debates on the gendering of subjectivity in feminist theory for it avoids both essentialism and hyperconstructivism.

Le Doeuff, Michèle (1989) *L'Etude et le rouet: Des femmes, de la philosophie, etc.* Paris: Seuil. (Trans. T. Selous, *Hipparchia's Choice: An Essay Concerning Women, Philosophy, etc.* (1991), Oxford, UK/Cambridge, MA: Blackwell.)
Important and witty study by a leading French philosopher examining women's relationship to philosophy, exemplified by the case of Beauvoir. Analyses the misogynist aspects of Sartre's philosophy and the differences between Beauvoir and Sartre's contributions to existentialism. Highly recommended.

Lilar, Suzanne (1969) *Le Malentendu du Deuxième Sexe*, Paris: PUF.
Early French feminist critique of *The Second Sex*.

Lundgren-Gothlin, Eva (1996) *Sex and Existence*, London: Athlone. (Edited trans. *Sexe et existence: La philosophie de Simone de Beauvoir* (2001) (trans. M. Kail), Paris: Michalon.)
Important study of the philosophical sources of *The Second Sex*. Essential reading.

Mahon, Joseph (1998) *Existentialism, Feminism and Simone de Beauvoir*, Basingstoke: Macmillan.
Accessible introduction to Beauvoir's ethics.

Marks, Elaine (ed.) (1987) *Critical Essays on Simone de Beauvoir*, Boston, MA: G. K. Hall.

Extensive and diverse collection of portraits, reviews, extracts and essays by important contributors such as Sartre, Francis Jeanson, Juliet Mitchell, Michèle Le Doeuff, Kate Millett and Alice Jardine among others.

Miller, Sarah Clark (2001) 'The lived experience of doubling: Simone de Beauvoir's phenomenology of old age', in W. O'Brien and L. Embree (eds) *The Existential Phenomenology of Simone de Beauvoir*, Dordrecht/Boston, MA/London: Kluwer Academic Publishers.

Clear philosophical overview of *Old Age*.

Moi, Toril (1990) *Feminist Theory and Simone de Beauvoir*, Oxford: Blackwell.

Contains two important essays on clichés in the reception of Beauvoir's work and on the short story, 'The woman destroyed'.

—— (1994) *Simone de Beauvoir: The Making of an Intellectual Woman*, Cambridge, MA/Oxford: Blackwell.

Groundbreaking sophisticated study of Beauvoir's intellectual trajectory and philosophical and literary writing from a combined feminist psychoanalytical and socio-historical approach. Intellectually provocative and essential reading.

—— (1999) *What is a Woman?* Oxford: Oxford University Press.

Important contribution to current debates in feminist theory, including two new essays on Beauvoir and *The Second Sex*. Essential reading.

O'Brien, Wendy and Embree, Lester (eds) (2001) *The Existential Phenomenology of Simone de Beauvoir*, Dordrecht/Boston, MA/London: Kluwer Academic Publishers.

Ten essays exploring the existential phenomenological aspects of Beauvoir's thought. Includes valuable bibliography of primary and secondary works. Philosophically demanding for the non-specialist reader.

Okely, Judith (1986) *Simone de Beauvoir: A Re-reading*, London: Virago.

Rereading of Beauvoir's writing by feminist social anthropologist, assessing its impact in the 1950s and early 1960s and the issues it raises for readers in the 1980s.

Patterson, Yolanda (1989) *Simone de Beauvoir and the Demystification of Motherhood*, Ann Arbor, MI/London: UMI Research Press.

Accessible study of motherhood in Beauvoir's writing.

Pilardi, Jo-Ann (1999) *Simone de Beauvoir, Writing the Self: Philosophy Becomes Autobiography*, Westport, CT/London: Praeger Publishers.

Philosophical reading of Beauvoir's notion of self in her philosophical and autobiographical writing. Accessible.

Rodgers, Catherine (1998) *Le Deuxième Sexe de Simone de Beauvoir, un héritage admiré et contesté*, Paris: L'Harmattan.

Collection of interviews with leading French feminists, including Christine Delphy, Julia Kristeva and Michèle Le Doeuff, assessing the impact of *The Second Sex*. Highly recommended.

Simons, Margaret A. (ed.) (1995) *Feminist Interpretations of Simone de Beauvoir*, University Park, PA: Pennsylvania State University Press.

Collection of interdisciplinary essays on Beauvoir's philosophical and literary writing, including one by French philosopher, Michèle Le Doeuff. Recommended.

——— (1999) *Beauvoir and The Second Sex: Feminism, Race and the Origins of Existentialism*, Lanham, MA/Oxford: Rowman and Littlefield.

Important collection of essays published from 1979–1988 by leading figure in Beauvoir studies, comprising three interviews with Beauvoir, studies of her feminism and philosophical writing, and her philosophical influence on Sartre. Essential reading.

Stefanson, Blandine (1980) 'Introduction to Simone de Beauvoir', *Les Belles Images*, London: Heinemann.

Critical introduction to *Les Belles Images* and useful interview with Beauvoir.

Tidd, Ursula (1999) *Simone de Beauvoir, Gender and Testimony*, Cambridge: Cambridge University Press.

Feminist study of Beauvoir's testimonial auto/biographical writings in the context of her notion of selfhood formulated in her ethical essays and in *The Second Sex*.

Vintges, Karen (1996) *Philosophy as Passion: The Thinking of Simone de Beauvoir*, Bloomington and Indianapolis, IN: Indiana University Press.

An accessible study of Beauvoir's philosophy and its relation to her life, drawing on Foucault's later ethics.

WORKS CITED

Note: works by Simone de Beauvoir that are cited in this book are listed in the 'Further Reading' section, pp. 127–142.

Al-Hibri, Azizah Y. and Simons, Margaret A. (eds) (1990) *Hypatia Reborn: Essay in Feminist Philosophy*, Bloomington and Indianapolis, IN: Indiana University Press.

Anderson, Bonnie S. and Zinsser, Judith P. (1990) *A History of Their Own: Women in Europe from Prehistory to the Present, Vol. II*, Harmondsworth: Penguin.

Bair, Deirdre (1990) *Simone de Beauvoir,* London: Jonathan Cape.

Barthes, Roland (1964) 'Ecrivants et écrivains', in *Essais critiques*, Paris: Seuil 'Tel Quel', pp. 147–154. (Translation 'Authors and writers', in Susan Sontag (ed.) *A Roland Barthes Reader* (1993), London: Vintage, pp. 185–193.)

Battersby, Christine (1989) *Gender and Genius: Towards a Feminist Aesthetics*, London: The Women's Press.

Bauer, Nancy (2001) *Simone de Beauvoir: Philosophy and Feminism*, New York: Columbia University Press.

Bennett, Joy and Hochmann, Gabriella (1988) *Simone de Beauvoir: An Annotated Bibliography,* New York and London: Garland Publishing.

Bergoffen, Deborah (1997) *The Philosophy of Simone de Beauvoir: Gendered Phenomenologies, Erotic Generosities*, New York: SUNY.

Butler, Judith (1986) 'Sex and gender in Simone de Beauvoir's *Second Sex*', in Hélène Wenzel (ed.) 'Simone de Beauvoir: Witness to a Century', *Yale French Studies* 72: 35–49.

—— (1987; reprint 1999) *Subjects of Desire: Hegelian Reflections in Twentieth-Century France*, New York: Columbia University Press.

—— (1990) *Gender Trouble, Feminism and the Subversion of Identity*, London and New York: Routledge.

Card, Claudia (ed.) (2003) *The Cambridge Companion to Simone de Beauvoir*, Cambridge: Cambridge University Press.

Coderre, Cécile and Tahon, Marie-Blanche (eds) (2001) *Le Deuxième Sexe: Une relecture en trois temps, 1949–1971–1999*, Montreal: Editions du Remue-Ménage.

Cooper, David E. (1999) *Existentialism*, Malden, MA/Oxford: Blackwell Publishers.

Daly, Mary (1968) *The Church and The Second Sex*, New York: Harper and Row.

Dayan, Josée and Ribowska, Malka (1979) *Simone de Beauvoir: un film*, Paris: Gallimard.

Delphy, Christine (1996) 'Rethinking sex and gender', in Diana Leonard and Lisa Adkins (eds) *Sex in Question: French Materialist Feminism*, London: Taylor & Francis, pp. 30–41.

—— and Chaperon, Sylvie (eds) (2002) *Cinquantenaire du Deuxième Sexe*, Paris: Syllepse.

Deutsch, Helene (1944) *The Psychology of Women*, New York: Grune and Stratton.

Duchen, Claire (1986) *Feminism in France, from May '68 to Mitterand*, London: Routledge.

Eagleton, Terry (1983) *Literary Theory*, Oxford: Blackwell.

Evans, Mary (1985) *Simone de Beauvoir: A Feminist Mandarin*, London: Tavistock.

—— (1996) *Simone de Beauvoir*, London: Sage.

Evans, Ruth (ed.) (1998) *Simone de Beauvoir's The Second Sex: New Interdisciplinary Essays*, Manchester: Manchester University Press.

Fallaize, Elizabeth (1988) *The Novels of Simone de Beauvoir*, London: Routledge.

—— (1993) *French Women's Writing: Recent Fiction*, Basingstoke: Macmillan.

—— (1998) *Simone de Beauvoir: A Critical Reader*, London and New York: Routledge.

Fanon, Frantz (1952) *Peau noire, Masques blancs*, Paris: Seuil. (Trans. Charles Lam Markmann, *Black Skin, White Masks* (1967), New York: Grove Weidenfeld.)

Firestone, Shulamith (1972) *The Dialectic of Sex*, London: Jonathan Cape.

Fishwick, Sarah (2002) *The Body in the Work of Simone de Beauvoir*, Oxford and New York: Peter Lang.

Forster, Penny and Sutton, Imogen (eds) (1989) *Daughters of de Beauvoir*, London: The Women's Press and Arts Council (film).

Francis, Claude and Gontier, Fernande (eds) (1979) *Les Ecrits de Simone de Beauvoir*, Paris: Gallimard.

Fraser, Mariam (1999) *Identity Without Selfhood*, Cambridge: Cambridge University Press.

Fullbrook, Kate and Fullbrook, Edward (1993) *Simone de Beauvoir and Jean-Paul Sartre: The Remaking of a Twentieth Century Legend*, Hemel Hempstead: Harvester Wheatsheaf.

—— (1998) *Simone de Beauvoir: A Critical Introduction*, Cambridge: Polity Press.

Gennari, Geneviève (1958) *Simone de Beauvoir*, Paris: Editions universi-taires.

Gothlin, Eva (1999) 'Simone de Beauvoir's notions of appeal, desire and ambiguity, and their relationship to Jean-Paul Sartre's notions of appeal and desire' in *Hypatia Special Issue 'The Philosophy of Simone de Beauvoir'* 14 (4): 83–95.

Gregory, Abigail and Tidd, Ursula (eds) (2000) *Women in Contemporary France*, Oxford/New York: Berg.

Grosz, Elizabeth (1989) *Sexual Subversions: Three French Feminists*, St Leonards, Australia: Allen and Unwin.

Gunther, Renate (1998) 'Fifty years on: the impact of Simone de Beauvoir's *Le Deuxième Sexe* on contemporary feminist theory', *Modern and Contemporary France* 6 (2): 177–188.

Haraway, Donna (1991) *Simians, Cyborgs and Women: The Reinvention of Nature*, London: Free Association Books.

Havelock Ellis, Henry (1897–1928) *Studies in the Psychology of Sex*, Philadelphia: F. A. Davis.

Hayward, Susan (1993) *French National Cinema*, London: Routledge.

Heath, Jane (1989) *Simone de Beauvoir*, Brighton: Harvester Wheatsheaf.

Hegel, G. W. F. (1977) *Phenomenology of Spirit* (trans. A. V. Miller), Oxford: Oxford University Press.

Heidegger, Martin (1962) *Being and Time* (trans. John MacQuarrie and Edward Robinson), New York: Harper and Row.

Heinämaa, Sara (1997) 'What is a woman? Butler and Beauvoir on the foundations of sexual difference', *Hypatia* 12 (1): 20–39.

Hekman, Susan J. (1990) *Gender and Knowledge: Elements of a Postmodern Feminism*, Cambridge: Polity Press.

Irigaray, Luce (1974) *Speculum, de l'autre femme*, Paris: Minuit. (Trans. G. Gill, *Speculum, of the Other Woman* (1985), Ithaca, NY: Cornell University Press.)

—— (1977) *Ce sexe qui n'en est pas un*, Paris: Minuit. (Trans. C. Porter with C. Burke, *This Sex Which is Not One* (1985), Ithaca, NY: Cornell University Press.)

—— (1995) 'The question of the other', in L. Huffer (ed.) 'Another Look, Another Woman', *Yale French Studies* 87: 7–19.

Jackson, Stevi (1996) *Christine Delphy*, London: Sage.

Jeanson, Francis (1966) *Simone de Beauvoir ou l'entreprise de vivre*, Paris: Seuil.

Kail, Michel (ed.) (2002) 'Présences de Simone de Beauvoir', *Les Temps Modernes*, 619: 5–252.

Keefe, Terry (1983) *Simone de Beauvoir: A Study of her Writings*, Totowa, NJ: Barnes and Noble.

Kristeva, Julia (1999–2002) *Le Génie feminine, tome 1: Hannah Arendt; tome 2: Melanie Klein; tome 3: Colette*, Paris: Fayard.

Kruks, Sonia (1990) *Situation and Human Existence: Freedom, Subjectivity and Society*, London: Unwin Hyman.

—— (1992) 'Gender and subjectivity: Simone de Beauvoir and contemporary feminism', *Signs* 18 (1): 89–110.

Lacan, Jacques (1938) 'Les Complexes familiaux dans la formation de l'individu: Essai d'analyse d'une fonction en psychologie' in *Encyclopédie Française*, Volume 8, Paris: Larousse, pp. 3–16. (Reprinted in 1984, Paris: Navarin.)

Le Doeuff, Michèle (1989) *L'Etude et le rouet: Des femmes, de la philosophie, etc.* Paris: Seuil. (Trans. T. Selous, *Hipparchia's Choice: An Essay Concerning Women, Philosophy, etc.* (1991), Cambridge, MA/Oxford: Blackwell.)

Lilar, Suzanne (1969) *Le Malentendu du Deuxième Sexe*, Paris: PUF.

Lundgren-Gothlin, Eva (1996) *Sex and Existence*, London: Athlone/Hanover, NH: Wesleyan University Press. (Edited trans. *Sexe et Existence: La Philosophie de Simone de Beauvoir* (2001), Paris: Michalon.)

Mahon, Joseph (1997) *Existentialism, Feminism and Simone de Beauvoir*, Basingstoke: Macmillan.

Marks, Elaine (1986) 'Transgressing the incontinent boundaries: the body in decline', *Yale French Studies* 72: 181–200.

Marks, Elaine (ed.) (1987) *Critical Essays on Simone de Beauvoir*, Boston: G. K. Hall.

Marx, Karl (1977) *Selected Writings*, ed. D. McLellan, Oxford: Oxford University Press.

Merleau-Ponty, Maurice (1962) *Phenomenology of Perception* (trans. C. Smith), London: Routledge. (First published as *Phénoménologie de la perception* (1945), Paris: Gallimard.)

—— (1964) 'Metaphysics and the novel', in *Sense and Non-sense* (trans. H. Dreyfus and P. Dreyfus), Evanston, IL: NorthWestern University

Press, pp. 26–40. (First published as 'Le roman et la métaphysique' (1948), in *Sens et non-sens*, Paris: Nagel, pp. 45–71.)

Mianda, Gertrude (2001) 'Le féminisme postcolonial et *Le Deuxième Sexe*: rupture ou continuité?', in Cécile Coderre and Marie-Blanche Tahon (eds) *Le Deuxième Sexe: Une relecture en trois temps, 1949–1971–1999*, Montreal: Editions du Remue-Ménage, pp. 143–160.

Miller, Sarah Clark (2001) 'The lived experience of doubling: Simone de Beauvoir's phenomenology of old age', in W. O'Brien and L. Embree (eds) *The Existential Phenomenology of Simone de Beauvoir*, Dordrecht/Boston, MA/London: Kluwer Academic Publishers.

—— (1994) *Simone de Beauvoir: The Making of an Intellectual Woman*, Cambridge, MA/Oxford: Blackwell.

—— (1999) *What is a Woman?* Oxford: Oxford University Press.

Moi, Toril (1990) *Feminist Theory and Simone de Beauvoir*, Oxford: Blackwell.

Mulvey, Laura (1975) 'Visual pleasure and narrative cinema', *Screen* 16 (3): 6–18.

Murdoch, Iris (1999) 'The existentialist hero', in Peter Conradi (ed.) *Existentialists and Mystics: Writings on Philosophy and Literature*, Harmondsworth: Penguin, pp. 108–115.

O'Brien, Wendy and Embree, Lester (eds) (2001) *The Existential Phenomenology of Simone de Beauvoir*, Dordrecht/Boston, MA/London: Kluwer Academic Publishers.

Okely, Judith (1986) *Simone de Beauvoir: A Re-reading*, London: Virago.

Patterson, Yolanda (1989) *Simone de Beauvoir and the Demystification of Motherhood*, Ann Arbor, MI/London: UMI Research Press.

Pilardi, Jo-Ann (1999) *Simone de Beauvoir, Writing the Self: Philosophy Becomes Autobiography*, Westport, CT/London: Praeger Publishers.

Ramazanoglu, Caroline (ed.) (1993) *Up Against Foucault*, London: Routledge.

Rich, Adrienne (1980) 'Compulsory heterosexuality and lesbian existence', *Signs* 5 (4): 631–660.

Rodgers, Catherine (1998) *Le Deuxième Sexe de Simone de Beauvoir: Un héritage admiré et contesté*, Paris: L'Harmattan.

Roudinesco, Elisabeth (1986) *La Bataille de cent ans: histoire de la psychanalyse en France, 2: 1925–1985*, Paris: Seuil. (Trans. Jeffrey Mehlman, *Jacques Lacan & Co.: A History of Psychoanalysis in France 1925–1985* (1990), London: Free Association Books.)

Sartre, Jean-Paul (1936) *La Transcendance de l'ego: Esquisse d'une description phénoménologique*, Paris: Vrin. (Trans. Forrest Williams and Robert Kirkpatrick, *The Transcendence of the Ego: An Existentialist Theory of Consciousness* (1965), New York: The Noonday Press.)

—— (1943) *L'Etre et le néant*, Paris: Gallimard. (Trans. Hazel E. Barnes, *Being and Nothingness* (1989), London: Routledge.)

—— (1946) *L'Existentialisme est un Humanisme*, Paris: Nagel. (Trans. P. Mairet, *Existentialism and Humanism* (1973), London: Methuen.)

—— (1948) *Qu'est-ce que la littérature?*, Paris: Gallimard. (Trans. Bernard Frechtman, *What is Literature?* (1950), London: Methuen.)

—— (1983) *Cahiers pour une morale*, Paris: Gallimard. (Trans. David Pellauer, *Notebooks for an Ethics* (1992), Chicago: University of Chicago Press.)

Schor, Naomi (1989) 'This essentialism which is not one: coming to grips with Irigaray', *Differences* 1 (2): 38–58.

Simons, Margaret A. (ed.) (1995) *Feminist Interpretations of Simone de Beauvoir*, University Park, PA: Pennsylvania State University Press.

—— (ed.) (1999) 'The philosophy of Simone de Beauvoir', *Hypatia: A Journal of Feminist Philosophy*, 14 (4).

—— (1999) *Beauvoir and The Second Sex: Feminism, Race and the Origins of Existentialism*, Lanham, MA/Oxford: Rowman and Littlefield.

Spurling, Laurie (1977) *Phenomenology and the Social World: The Philosophy of Merleau-Ponty and its Relation to the Social Sciences*, London: Routledge.

Stefanson, Blandine (1980) *Introduction to Simone de Beauvoir, Les Belles Images*, London: Heinemann.

Tidd, Ursula (1999) *Simone de Beauvoir, Gender and Testimony*, Cambridge: Cambridge University Press.

——— (2002) 'Le Deuxième Sexe, la conscience noire et la conscience lesbienne', in C. Delphy and S. Chaperon (eds) *Cinquantenaire du Deuxième Sexe*, Paris: Editions Syllepse.

Vintges, Karen (1996) *Philosophy as Passion: The Thinking of Simone de Beauvoir*, Bloomington and Indianapolis, IN: Indiana University Press.

Warnock, Mary (1970) *Existentialism*, Oxford: Oxford University Press.

Warren, Denise (1987) 'Beauvoir on Bardot: the ambiguity syndrome', *Dalhousie French Studies* 13: 39–50.

Wenzel, Hélène V. (ed.) (1986) 'Simone de Beauvoir: Witness to a Century', *Yale French Studies* 72.

Wittig, Monique (1992) *The Straight Mind*, Hemel Hempstead: Harvester Wheatsheaf.

INDEX